CONTENTS

LANGUAGE IN FOCUS

New Edition

A GUIDE TO COMPREHENDING AND COMPOSING

Leaving Certificate English *Higher Level*

JOHN SHEIL

Published by
CJ Fallon
Ground Floor – Block B
Liffey Valley Office Campus
Dublin 22

First edition March 2013
This reprint September 2013

Printed in Ireland by
Turner Print Group
Earl Street
Longford

Acknowledgements

The publishers and author gratefully acknowledge the following who have granted permission to reproduce copyright material: David Higham Associates for extract from Stephen Fry, *Moab is my Washpot*; AP Watt (United Agents) for extract from Brenda Maddox, *The Real Life of Molly Bloom/ Nora Joyce*; Faber & Faber for extract from PD James, *The Children of Men*; Liberties Press for Con Houlihan's 'More than a Game'; *Irish Times*, *Irish Independent*; *The Guardian*; Hodder Headline Ireland for extract from Ruairi Quinn, *Straight Left*; Kevin Williams; John O'Keeffe; Gaius Coffey; Vona Groarke; Wolfhound Press for extract from Gabriel Byrne, *Pictures in my Head*; Xenophobe's Guides Ltd for extract from Frank McNally, *The Xenophobe's Guide to the Irish*.

Every effort has been made to secure permission to reproduce copyright material in this book. However, if the publishers have inadvertently overlooked any copyright holders, they will be pleased to come to a suitable arrangement with them at the earliest opportunity.

INTRODUCTION

OBJECTIVES OF THIS BOOK

"The syllabus should provide opportunities for the development of higher-order thinking skills of analysis, inference, synthesis and evaluation...Also, students' knowledge and level of control of the more formal aspects of language, e.g. register, paragraphs, syntax, punctuation and spelling, should be given particular attention..."

"The study of thinking skills and language is emphasised throughout...Students will be expected to see every language product, whether it be a memo or a poem, a political speech or a play, as a text which needs to be studied and its specific genre understood."

— Leaving Certificate English Syllabus

The aim of this new edition of *Language in Focus* is to help students develop the reading and writing skills that are needed in order to become effective, accurate and creative users of language.

The primary focus is on **Comprehending** and **Composing**.

This book has a dual purpose:

1. **To develop the reading skills of students.**

   The comprehension texts have been chosen with the demands and interests of students in mind. It is the author's belief that people write best when they are interested in a topic. The wide-ranging content of the texts, written in a variety of styles, should appeal to the active and inquisitive minds of Leaving Certificate students. Newspaper articles, speeches, stories, advertisements, visuals, diaries and reports are offered to show students the multifaceted approach to language that is encouraged by the Leaving Certificate syllabus.

   It is hoped that students will engage with the texts. Questions have been designed with the aim of encouraging skills of comprehension, understanding, interpretation and analysis that will guide a critical response.

2. **To develop the writing skills of students.**

   The most important response that students can make to a text is the written one. The texts chosen serve as creative models through which students can develop their own responses.

   Effective and creative writing is the most important skill required by Paper One. This book offers plenty of practical advice that will enable students to write in a variety of ways from the practical to the creative. Numerous examples of Functional Writing and Composing are given, which should serve as models and inspiration for students' own original work.

This book will help students to become:

- Perceptive readers.
- Efficient writers.

Students must be excited by what they read before they can give their own responses in an effective and meaningful manner. The comprehension texts should act as stimuli for written work. Each exercise that a student attempts should be guided by a clear sense of purpose and of audience, and should be delivered in a language suited to the task.

The Leaving Certificate examination puts a special emphasis on composition and this is reflected in the space given to this skill in the book.

STRUCTURE

This book has been written in an ordered and structured manner, so that students can learn the skills that the syllabus requires.

Section One is an introduction to tools of language – the foundation stones of written English. Students should not neglect the mechanics of the language they use. The essential elements of language cannot be learnt in a few lessons, but – by reminding students of their importance – it is hoped that these can be instilled during the senior years of secondary school.

Section Two is a thorough examination of comprehension. The aim is to help students develop critical skills of **reading**, **comprehending**, **evaluating** and **responding**.

The extracts are challenging but also, hopefully, will encourage students to develop their own reading. The reading of newspaper articles, novels and biographies/autobiographies should be encouraged for all Leaving Certificate students, as these will help in the acquisition of language. Much emphasis is placed on the stylistic aspects of comprehension passages. The discerning reader will learn how language works.

Section Three is focused on functional writing. The examples are chosen from students' work and from the work of professional writers. Clear guidelines are outlined, which will aid students in their own attempts to write effectively.

Section Four is devoted to composition. This is the most important area examined in the Leaving Certificate, but is often one for which students are least prepared. The skills needed for composing are learnt over a long time. With practice and application, these skills can be developed and, in time, students will become adept at expressing themselves in a fluent manner.

Finally, Section Five provides advice on the examination itself. The advice is accompanied by the Criteria of Assessment, so that teachers and students are made aware of how scripts are marked. Tips on timing and approaches to answering are offered.

Remember that Paper One is a test of skills not knowledge. The skills of Comprehending and Composing are honed over a number of years. I hope that this book will help students to become effective, rational and sensitive users of English.

The English language skills that you learn will enrich all aspects of your future life – academic and working – and will enable you to be a more discerning reader and more effective writer of English.

SECTION 1
LANGUAGE

1 TOOLS OF LANGUAGE

INTRODUCTION

This chapter will examine:

- **Register**
- **Parts or components of speech**
- **Spelling**
- **Punctuation**
- **Sentences and paragraphs**
- **Drafting**
- **How to improve your writing**

Before we begin, it is worth remembering the key fact that **we use language and writing to communicate and to be understood**. To communicate effectively, some understanding of how language functions is necessary. This chapter will examine the words we use and how we arrange them into sentences and paragraphs. Some knowledge of grammar and punctuation is necessary if we are to write well and with clarity. An awareness of how language functions will enable the user of it to be more effective.

This chapter outlines the basic rules of **grammar**, **punctuation** and **word usage**.

Writing is a skill that takes time and patience to develop. It is worth developing this skill because it will be with you for the rest of your life.

READ REGULARLY

The first step you should take is to set aside time for reading on a daily basis. This will help to expand your vocabulary. If possible, read novels, biographies and autobiographies. If you have a special interest in movies or sport, read books on these topics. Every Leaving Certificate student should read newspapers regularly. This will open you up to the world around you. Over time, reading widely will result in an expanded vocabulary. You will have a greater appreciation of facts and opinion.

USE A DICTIONARY AND THESAURUS

REGISTER

Register is the language appropriate to a particular topic, situation and/or audience.

The following examples show what happens when the language used is not in the correct register. The result is awkward expression.

1. Hamlet is a bit of a nutter. In his long speeches, he seems sane enough, but then he does crazy things. But you'd kinda feel for him. I prefer him to the other dude, Laertes, who acts way over the top when he hears that his dad has been wasted by Hamlet and his sister has gone doo-lally.

2. Dear Sir,
   I wish to register a complaint about the Digital Versatile Disc (DVD) player that I purchased at your wonderful emporium. The apparatus is not functioning as intended. I implore you to act with celerity on this matter and furnish me with a reimbursement.
   Most humbly yours
   St John Percival Appleplum

3. Yo God, things ain't so cool with me. I don't feel the love of my bros just now. I need some of that awesome power that you got in truckloads. Shine some of that goodness this way and I will pay my dues to you. Thanks, man.

4. This product is only great. Do yourself a favour – buy it. Your life will be transformed. Our company will be enriched and the share price will soar. Believe me, it's worth spending a little extra on this one.

5. The display of this Irish team is truly splendiferous. The Irish midfield is passing the ball with the grace and poise of Russian ballerinas; our backs are engaged in Herculean endeavours; while our forwards are executing Wagnerian manoeuvres.

EXERCISES

1. Match the above examples with the following:
   (a) Letter of complaint
   (b) Essay on a Shakespearean play
   (c) Prayer
   (d) Football commentary
   (e) Advertisement
2. Examine each in terms of register, purpose, tone and audience.
3. Assess the appropriateness of the language used in each example.
4. Rewrite each one in a more effective way.

INFORMAL REGISTER

TEXT MESSAGES

Text messaging is an example of communication that uses an **informal register**.

The widespread use of mobile phones has given us a new and dynamic means of communicating. Sending text messages is fast and cheap. Messages are short because of the limited space available, but a system of abbreviated words and symbols has been developed. This is ideal for short informal communication, but texting is not suitable for all situations. For example, it would be inappropriate to end a relationship with a text message.

Try to translate the following into conventional English:

- *Wil u pik me up @ haf4*
- *RU goin 2da flm with any1?*
- *CU 2mro at skool.*
- *Wan2 spk b4 2late.*

While text messaging is acceptable in its own context, these shortcuts with language should never be used in situations that demand a more formal form of writing. Another problem with texting is that there is not universal agreement as to the meaning of each abbreviation. This results in this form of language communication having a lack of clarity.

SLANG

Slang is informal language usually associated with young people or with specific groups in society. Slang is designed to include those who are in the know but it excludes others. Examples include the following:

- *Minging, legend, random, ace*
- *Whistle and flute* (suit in Cockney rhyming slang)

DIALECT

Dialect is language specific to a region and is considered to be informal. Examples include the following:

- *wee* = small (Scotland and the north of Ireland)
- *sarnies* = sandwiches (North of England)
- *bazzer* = haircut (Cork)
- *to mitch* = to play truant (*bunk off*) from school (Dublin)

Slang and dialect can be used to reflect the vibrant language of a specific group of users, but should be avoided if your intention is to be widely understood.

COLLOQUIAL LANGUAGE

Colloquial language is the relaxed, informal language of everyday conversation. This is how we communicate with family and friends. Examples include the following:

- *I bumped into this bloke today.*
- *Isn't it just great having a free day tomorrow?*

CLICHÉS

Cliches can be described as worn-out phrases. They are ineffective because they have become overused. Examples include the following:

- *I'm glad you asked me.*
- *Wait until you have kids of your own.*

- *It's a game of two halves.*
- *A blanket of snow covered the ground.*
- *At the end of the day, someone will have to bury the hatchet.*
- *Going forward, we all have to tighten our belts.*

FORMAL REGISTER

The **formal register** is used when we wish to communicate in an impersonal manner. It is polite and respectful language. Examples include the following:

- *Good afternoon, ladies and gentlemen, please be up standing...*
- *Your Honour, I can assure you that I will not offend again.*

Can you guess the context of the two sentences above? This is possible because they involve formal phrases that are always used in particular contexts. Other examples of the formal register are used in everyday situations:

- *Good evening, Mr Brennan, can I help you?*
- *My name is Mary Duffy and I would like to apply for...*

The formal register is often used in Leaving Certificate compositions. An essay on a Shakespearean play, for example, is generally best expressed in formal language. Remember that the language should feel right.

Business letters and **reports** are cases of written texts that use a **formal register**. Note the **layout** of formal reports and letters, as in the following example:

Dear Sir/Madam,
This is to inform you that your rent is now overdue.
Please pay the requisite amount at your earliest convenience.
Yours sincerely,
Patrick R. Lombard

Language as Clothes

You might like to imagine language as clothes. It is acceptable to wear jeans and a hoodie when meeting casually with friends, but not if you are attending a job interview or a wedding. Sometimes, informal language (casual dress) is simply inappropriate.

COMMON REGISTER

The **common register** is ordinary language that is neutral in tone. We use this to write letters to the newspapers, to put forth ideas in personal essays, and so on.

The following comparative lists should help you to distinguish between the informal, formal and common registers.

INFORMAL	COMMON	FORMAL
hi	hello	good day
gaff	house	domicile
wheels	car	vehicle
wicked	fantastic	remarkable
nick	steal	misappropriate

EXERCISES

1. Compile a short user's guide to texting for the beginner.
2. (a) Write a short dialogue in which two Leaving Certificate students discuss their weekend. Include examples of slang in your dialogue. Underline the slang words and expressions.

   (b) Give an explanation of the most obscure terms.
3. Match the following sentences with a country or region:
   (a) *I cannae remember the bairn's name. Oh aye, the things I do remember, is he couldnae forgit nothing.*

   (b) *It's like so dangerous on the Dart.*

   (c) *Where would you be going in that? It's far from fancy outfits you were brought up to dress in?*

   (d) *I would just like to say that this cup of tea is frightfully hot but the scones are absolutely spiffing.*

   (e) *Hey, mate, nice whistle you got there. The oul' trouble get it for you then?*

   (f) *Are you lookin' at me? Oh, I see. A wise guy, eh? Take a hike before the cops arrive.*
4. Read the following extract from Roddy Doyle's novel *The Van*. The novel is set in Dublin during Italia '90, when the whole country was captivated by the performance of our soccer team. Comment on the register. Underline the words and phrases that are colloquial and give a more formal equivalent.

SOCCER MAD

The country had gone soccer mad. Oul'ones were explaining offside to each other; the young ones at the check-out in the cash-and-carry told Jimmy Sr that Romania hadn't a hope cos Locatus was suspended because he was on two yellow cards. It was great. There were flags hanging out of nearly every window in Barrytown. It was great for business as well. There were no proper dinners being made at all. Half the mammies were watching the afternoon matches, and after the extra-time and the penalty shoot-outs there was no time to make the dinner before the next match. The whole place was living on chips.

5. Compile a short list of clichéd phrases that might be used when writing about:
   (a) sport
   (b) politics

Get the register right!

Adapt your language to the audience and the subject.

6. Read the following tasks and choose one. In your answer, pay particular attention to the language you use in connecting with your audience.

   (a) As a senior student, you have been asked to write a speech welcoming and advising a group of First Years on their first day in secondary school.

   (b) Write a letter to a national newspaper on an educational issue about which you feel strongly.

(c) You are spending a week away from home; write an e-mail to your parents giving details of a problem you are experiencing.

(d) Your mobile phone has been confiscated; write a letter to your Year Head in which you explain the circumstances of how this happened and offer an apology.

(e) Introduce (by means of a speech) a famous person to your school assembly.

PARTS OF SPEECH

It is essential that you know each of the following parts or components of speech that are dealt with in this section. You must understand the nuts and bolts of language in order to be able to write effectively.

NOUN

The **noun** names a person, place or thing. Examples are:

- cat, week, month, year, country, woman, ghost, ship, car

Remember that **proper nouns** (names of specific people and places) must begin with a **capital** letter.

- Gary, Sandra, Murphy, O'Kelly, Trim, Cairo, Africa, Mars
- Liffey, Mississippi, Everest, Monday, February

Common nouns are either concrete or abstract. Common nouns refer to things you can see or touch such as cat, window, school and player.

Abstract nouns are things you cannot see or touch. Examples of these are beauty, justice, appetite and fame.

Nouns can be **singular** or **plural**:

- Car/cars, telephone/s, book/s

Sometimes, the **plural** is not formed by simply adding an '**s**'.

- man/men
- child/children
- story/stories
- bus/buses
- mouse/mice
- sheep/sheep

Test yourself by writing out the correct plural of the following: leaf; hero; donkey; tomato; fish; country; stadium; knife.

PRONOUN

The **pronoun** substitutes a **noun**.

- *He* is sitting on the chair.
- *They* have no business being here.
- *I* am very glad you did that.
- What did *you* do with *it*?

VERB

The **verb** expresses **action**, **being** or **condition**.

- The dog *skidded* on the recently washed floor.
- Fortune *favours* the brave.
- The ghost *appeared* to the night watchmen.
- They *are* fortunate people.

The **tense** indicates when the action happens (past, present, future).

- Yesterday, I *drank* two litres of water.
- He only *drinks* strong coffee.
- I *am drinking* this very slowly.
- I *have drunk* that brand of cola.
- I *will drink* more milk in the future.

The subject and verb must be in agreement.

If the subject is singular, the singular form of the verb must be used.

- *The **man goes** to the cinema.* (note singular)
- *The **women go** to the theatre.* (note plural)

EXERCISES

1. **Fill the space with the correct form of the verb:**
   (a) Each of his books (*is/are*) new.
   (b) John's books (*is/are*) tattered and torn.
   (c) Latin (*was/were*) a requirement for entry to university.
   (d) Greek and Latin (*is/are*) studied in very few schools.
   (e) Tony and Sandra (*is/are*) studying.
   (f) I (*drink/drinks*) tea. He (*drink/drinks*) coffee. You (*drink/drinks*) milk. We all (*drink/drinks*) water.
2. **Are the verbs used correctly/incorrectly in the following sentences?**
   (a) Many writers *address* the theme of mortality in their work.
   (b) Everyone *agree* that telling lies is wrong.
   (c) The team *is doing* well at the moment.
   (d) The players *celebrate* victory by doing a lap of honour.
   (e) Every year, thousands of fish *is killed* by pollution.
   (f) Each person *is deserving* of respect.
   (g) The government *are elected* by the people.
   (h) The animals' cages *are* dirty.

Vary your verbs.

Look for **appropriate synonyms** to avoid repetition. Aim for accuracy of expression.

ADJECTIVE AND ADVERB

Adjectives and **adverbs** add description to your writing.

- **Adjectives** modify (add description to) a noun, e.g. the *heavy* box, the *tall* boy.
- Adjectives can have two further forms.
- The **comparative** form is used to compare two things – John is *taller* than Dave.
- The **superlative** form is used when more than two things or people are compared or to show that one has more of a quality than all of the others – Mark is the *tallest* boy.

Adverbs modify (add description to) a verb, an adjective or another adverb, e.g. glanced *secretly, very* heavy box, walked *too slowly.*

EXERCISES

Read these extracts and insert the missing adverbs and adjectives. You can choose from the lists under the passages.

1. The Reading Room

Adam crawled ....into the Reading Room just as the bell .... announced that the Library would close in fifteen minutes. As he sank on to his ....seat everyone around him began packing up, pushing back their chairs, yawning, stretching, sorting their papers and arranging their books. Many of them had been there all day: their countenances were ....but contented, conveying the satisfaction of work well done – so many books read, so ....notes taken. Then there were the Night People of the Museum – those writing books or theses while holding down ....jobs. Hurrying from their offices to the Museum through the rush-hour, pausing only to snatch a .... meal at Lyons, they worked through the evening with ....concentration. Now they looked ....at the clock, and continued reading even as they stood in line to return their books. Adam felt an imposter in this company, especially when they stood ....aside as he carried his huge, tottering pile of unread Lawrentiana to the ....counter.

(*The British Museum is Falling Down* by David Lodge)

(stridently, respectfully, fierce and greedy, padded, reproachfully, quick, fatigued, central, many, wearily, day-time)

2. The Ghost

The Ghost was not ....but his face was unusual. Pale as milk and slightly........., its features might have been stolen from several ....men. His nose was bent and a little too......... His ears protruded ....like those of a harlequin. His hair, as a ....overgrown black dandelion, might once have belonged to a pantomime ghoul. His ....eyes had an unearthly clarity which made the rest of his face seem .... despite its pallor. A smell of ....ashes hung around him, commingling with the odour of the long-time traveller. Yet he was more careful than many in his habits and was ....observed to use half his rations to wash his ....hair, as meticulous as any debutante preparing for a ball.

(*Star of the Sea* by Joseph O'Connor)

(frequently, dark, slightly, different, comically tangled, wet, elongated, long, hideously, ugly, wan)

PREPOSITION

The **preposition** shows a relationship between two things in a sentence.

- The very quiet neighbours live *at* Number four.
- Joan lives *across* the street.
- I like this house better *than* the other one.

Never end a sentence with a preposition unless it is completely unavoidable or sounds awkward. To paraphrase Winston Churchill: "Poor grammar is something up with which I will not put."

EXERCISES

Fill in the blanks with the appropriate preposition:

1. Denise removed the phone ________ her bag and put it ________ the table.
2. He left home ________ noon and returned ________ tea.
3. He put the hat ________ his head but the wind blew it ________.
4. He folded the newspaper ________ a scroll and used it to crush the fly ________ the wall.
5. ________ whom did you receive this parcel?
6. Bill went ________ the dance ________ Jenny, but he talked ________ his friends all evening.
7. You are ________ no obligation to buy this product.
8. There is a cat ________ the chair playing ________ a piece of string.
9. We were beaten ________ the better team; their players were psyched ________ the match.
10. There was someone standing ________ of me, I couldn't see ________ him.
11. I was frightened during the storm and hid ________ the blankets.
12. ________ the street there is a strange house ________ any doors or windows.

CONJUNCTION

The **conjunction** joins words, phrases or clauses. The italicised words in the following sentences are very common examples:

- He is both rich *and* friendly.
- I would go to their party *but* I am studying on Friday.
- Would you like tea *or* coffee?

EXERCISES

Fill in the blanks with the appropriate conjunctions:

1. You cannot get a decent suit for love ________ money.
2. You can choose one ________ the other.
3. I will answer your questions ________ I do not want to waste precious time.

4. I __________ want to see you __________ hear you again this evening.
5. I am __________ amazed __________ disgusted by your behaviour.
6. I was going to give you a present __________ I have changed my mind.

SENTENCES

A sentence is the **complete expression** of an idea or thought. All sentences:

- Begin with a capital letter.
- End with a full stop, question mark or exclamation mark.
- Are composed of a subject and a verb.

The word order of a sentence is called the **syntax** and is very important.

Subject – Verb – Object
The man has a cat.
The cat has a man.
The has a cat man.

The first two sentences in the box above mean very different things. The third does not make sense.

Awkward syntax is often the sign of careless writing.

For example:

- *Shakespeare, in the final act of Hamlet, brings the action to an exciting climax.*

This would be more effective if written:

- *In the final act of Hamlet, Shakespeare brings the action to an exciting climax.*

The subject of a sentence should be as close to the main verb as possible. In the following cliché, the order of the words changes the meaning:

- *Fail to prepare; prepare to fail.*

EXERCISES

Reassemble the jumbled words below into coherent sentences. Then rearrange the sentences into the correct sequence.

1. (a) prepare • the best • secondly • fishermen • themselves • eventualities • for • all
   (b) nothing caught • lastly • when • there is • the fisherman's • it is never • fault
   (c) about fishing • three important • there are • facts • to know
   (d) optimists • all fishermen • firstly • are
2. (a) should play football • her parents • that an Asian girl • do not think
   (b) passion for soccer • tells the story • Bend It Like Beckham • of one girl's
   (c) for a girls' team • when they hear • they are outraged • that she is playing
   (d) to anyone • with a sense of humour • recommend • I • it

3. (a) ensures • at any time of year • Ireland • the mild climate • that • secondly • can be visited

   (b) cultural activities • and • firstly • so many • there are • sporting • for • partake • tourist • in • the • throughout the year • to

   (c) the • Ireland • is • adventurous • for • tourist • an ideal destination

   (d) know • their guests • thirdly • Irish • the • how • treat • to

4. (a) until • in hospital • consciousness • didn't • she • she • up • regain • woke

   (b) as • falling • happened • was • accident • the • night

   (c) got • parked • drive • and • she • in • car • her • of • out • the

   (d) her • safely • happy • bed • family • gathered • entire • see • her • to • was • around • she

   (e) house • explosion • an • ripped • suddenly • through • the

   (f) coming • upstairs • from • Mrs. • house • approaching • Browne • saw • was • her • when • smoke • she • an • room

   (g) it • to • out • she • and • threw • blacked • of • the • her • force • ground • the

Always read over your work to check for grammatical errors. Most will be spotted immediately because poor expression often reads awkwardly.

SPELLING

Some Tips on Spelling

- Make it a habit to use a dictionary – do not guess the spellings of words of which you are unsure.
- Learn the correct spelling of the names of writers and their works that you are studying.
- Make a list of words that give you problems. Add to this list regularly.
- Eliminate spelling problems by learning off by heart.
- Remember that English spelling is uneven.
- Remember that most of the rules have exceptions.

We learn to recognise correct spelling by our practical use of them in reading and writing.

'**i**' before '**e**' except after '**c**'
Examples: die, friend, priest, deceive, receive, perceive
Some exceptions: society, efficient

Changing the form of verbs

Typical examples:

Love = loving
Take = taking
Run = running
Walk = walking

Give the following '**-ing**' endings:

Come
Make

Hop
Hope
Bounce
Cross
Write

PLURALS

Most **plurals** in English are formed by **adding** an '**s**'.
Examples:

cat/cats
book/books
chimp/chimps
darling/darlings

There are **exceptions**, as, for example, for the sibilant '**s**' sound.
Examples:

class/classes
wish/wishes
arch/arches
bus/buses
box/boxes

Beware of **odd** words. Look at the following examples:

fish/fish (but, if they are different species, then it is *fishes*)
deer/deer
medium/media
stadium/stadia

Words **ending** in a '**y**' should also be treated carefully:

boy/boys
toy/toys
bay/bays

The **exception** is when there is a **consonant** before the '**y**':

history/histories
spy/spies
story/stories

Words **ending** with '**o**' often simply take an '**s**':

photo/photos

But there are many exceptions:

hero/heroes
potato/potatoes
tomato/tomatoes

Homonyms are often confused and this leads to misspelling.

EXERCISES

Fill in the blanks using the appropriate word:

1. Their/they're/there
   ________ books are over ________, where ________ safe.

   ________ going ________ on ________ holidays with ________ families.

2. advise(v) advice(n)
   My mother gave me useful ________.

   I ________ her to work as hard as she can.

3. Quiet/quite
   It is very ________ in here.

   The room is ________ hot.

4. Accept/except
   Do you ________ my apology?

   I ________ all apologies ________ those that are not meant.

5. Taught/thought
   I ________ of something that might help.

   I was ________ to be well-behaved.

6. Threw/through
   I ________ the stone as far as I could.

   The stone went ________ the window.

7. Weather/whether
   The ________ is good for this time of year.

   I don't care ________ it is cold or not.

8. Principal/principle
   The only ________ worth following is the golden rule.

   Our ________ is very strict.

9. Past/passed
   Harriet ________ the note to Luke.

   John went ________ Lucy's house on the way home.

10. To/too
    I want you ________ address the letter ________ my boss.

    There is ________ much ________ do.

    Can I do it ________?

11. Were/where
    ________ ________ you last night?

    We ________ standing outside without a ticket.

12. Lose/loose
    The strings are ________ on this guitar.

    Did you ________ the plectrum?

LIST OF AWKWARD SPELLINGS

Here is a list of tricky words drawn up by Irish Leaving Certificate students:

accommodation
achievement
alcohol
amateur
argument
athlete
audience
beginning
believe
business
changeable
character
coarse
complementary
committed
complimentary
condemn
conscience
conscious
course
criticism
deceive
decision
definitely
describe
develop
disappoint
dissimilar
efficient

embarrass
environment
especially
existence
experience
extremely
fascinating
February
fierce
finally
foreign
genius
government
heroes
hospital
humorous
hygiene
hypocrisy
immediately
immigration
influence
interesting
irrelevant
knowledge
library
literature
loose
lose
marriage

meant
naïve
necessary
noticeable
omitted
opinion
opportunity
original
parallel
parliament
particularly
personal
personnel
pastime
pleasant
practice (noun)
practise (verb)
prejudice
privilege
probably
queue
really
receive
reference
religious
repetition
restaurant
rhyme
rhythm

science
sense
separate
Shakespeare
sincerely
skilful
society
soliloquy
strength
success
sympathy
taught
thoroughly
thought
through
tragedy
tragic
truly
unnecessary
usually
valuable
vengeance
vicious
villain
Wednesday
weird
wholly
writing
yacht

PUNCTUATION

Punctuation allows the writer to direct the tone of a piece of writing. In simple terms, punctuation marks tell us where to pause, stop, emphasise, lower or heighten our voices. They are like messages from the writer to the reader as to how the reading should be done.

Careful use of punctuation can change the meaning of sentences.

A woman, without her man, is nothing.
A woman: without her, man is nothing.

Examine this mini-dialogue:

John: Good morning.
Greg: Good morning?
John: Good. Morning.
Greg: Good morning!

Punctuation marks enable us to read effectively. Tone is affected and modified by their use. They also help to clarify meaning.

Study these sentences:

The girl's book is missing.
The girls' book is missing.
The girl's books are missing.
The girls' books are missing.

Explain the meaning of each of the above

THE FULL STOP

The full stop normally signals the end of a sentence. Always begin a new sentence with a capital letter.

The full stop is also often used in abbreviations:

- U.N., R.T.E., R.S.V.P

Recent trends, however, indicate that full stops are increasingly being omitted in some abbreviations.

As a rule, a full stop should be inserted when the final letter of the abbreviation is not the final letter of the full-length unabbreviated word. For example:

- Rev. for 'Reverend'.

However, when the final letter of the abbreviation is the same as the final letter of the full-length word, the current trend is to omit the full stop. For example:

- Mr for 'Mister'.

THE COMMA

Commas are also used to mark a pause in a sentence.

- *Yesterday, we studied the finer points of grammar, but we didn't watch the video.*
- *The lesson, surprisingly, was interesting.*

Commas are often used to signify a relative clause.

- *The teacher, who was only filling in for the day, managed to make grammar interesting.*
- *The new teacher is from Pittsburg, where she grew up.*

They are also used to separate words in a list.

- *Tomorrow, you will need books, pens and paper.*
- *The lesson is interesting, challenging, difficult and rewarding.*
- *You are going to read, write, watch and listen.*

In description, they can be used to separate adjectives.

- *It was a thundery, wet, clammy afternoon.*
- *The meal was healthy, tasty and inexpensive.*

APOSTROPHE

There are two main uses for the apostrophe:

1. To show ownership.

- *This is Miss Browne's video.*
- *This is Miss's book.*
- *This is the man's phone.*
- *This is the men's club.*
- *This is the team's pitch.*
- *These are the dogs' kennels.*
- *The child's bike.*
- *The children's bikes.*

EXCEPTIONS
its
his
hers
ours
yours

2. To indicate where there is a letter omitted.

- *She's going to be annoyed if you don't learn your grammar.*
- *I'm sure she wouldn't mind if we get the odd one wrong.*
- *I didn't do my written work; we've a test every week.*
- *It's not fair; they're always asking difficult questions.*
- *Who's the best at spelling in your class?*

INVERTED COMMAS

Inverted commas are also called quotation marks.
Double inverted commas are used in direct speech to indicate the exact words spoken.

"What punctuation mark is used to indicate a question?" asked Miss Kelly.
"I don't know," replied Susan.
"I do hope," Miss Kelly said, "that you will know the correct answer by the end of the week."

NOTE
Inverted commas enclose the exact words spoken, including the relevant punctuation marks.

You should use a new line to indicate a new speaker:

John said: "This time we will win."
"I am not so sure about that," Neasa replied.
"Of course we will!" John exclaimed, "Our debaters are on fire this weekend."

Inverted commas are also used when you quote from a text.

- *According to John Lord, in his book* Cycling to Hell, *"The bicycles go at the speed of light."*

If you do not use the full quotation, you can use ellipsis (…) to indicate that words have been left out:

- *"And…to thy own self be true."*

Single inverted commas are used to indicate the titles of short stories, e.g. 'Eveline'.

This type of inverted comma can be used to highlight a word or phrase.

- *The word 'anyways' is really annoying.*
- *Our 'state of the art' school is rat-infested and over-crowded.*

EXCLAMATION MARK

Exclamation marks are used to express surprise, fear or other strong emotions. They should be deployed infrequently.

- That's incredible!
- Whatever!

COLON and SEMICOLON

The colon introduces a list or a quotation or a comment.

- *She said: "Remember there will be a test on Friday."*
- *To succeed in any enterprise, you need the following: determination, knowledge and luck.*
- *Today, the teacher told us something really surprising: he, it seems, is a terrible speller.*

The semicolon is less strong than a full stop, but stronger than a comma.

- *Susan studied every weekend; otherwise, she was a normal teenager*

The semicolon can be used to separate phrases in a list to avoid confusion.

- *On our school trip, we visited Stratford-Upon-Avon; attended two plays; participated in a drama workshop; had a picnic near Anne Hathaway's house; and went on a guided tour of Shakespeare's house.*

EXERCISES

Punctuate the following:

1. gary can i have a loan of your copy of mice and men asked amanda of course replied gary but make sure you return it on Monday
2. what do the following have in common asked frank london berlin athens moscow melbourne sydney seoul and munich oh i know this one answered wendy they all hosted the olympic games isnt that correct yes its correct replied frank
3. where is your nokia shouted james mother its on the desk he replied calmly no its not she said getting angrier well then i dont know where it is he answered slowly dont take that tone with me young man she thundered i must have left it on the bus he said
4. whats your favourite subject at school jims aunt julie asked him while sipping her tea oh english of course he replied oh really she said what play are you studying macbeth he replied i know that one i studied it in school when i was a little girl my favourite bit was the is this a dagger i see before me speech his aunt said getting quite carried away
5. mum mindys bell is gone again said sally oh not again acknowledged her mother thats five this month dont worry mum ill go to the shop on larrys bike and get a new one replied sally youll do no such thing sallys mother said sternly that silly cat will just have to be more careful its not its fault said sally theres a perfectly good explanation well id like to

know her mother demanded well dont laugh at me but im sure the boys next door steal them whispered sally youre being silly sallys mother said impatiently and went indoors

6. ivan who was rather new in the country sat in the corridor trying to figure out the new timetable can i help asked sorcha when she noticed his puzzled expression yes thank you replied ivan i cant understand what lecture we have on wednesday nothings on Wednesday its st patrricks day weve no lectures expained sorcha thats great ivan said excitedly ill be able to sort out my notes clean my flat and go to the cinema whats on asked sorcha theres a polish film on in galway explained ivan its got subtitles maybe youd like to come along he asked id love to sorcha replied ok ill meet you at café connaught at half past seven said a delighted ivan

THE SENTENCE

A sentence is a group of words that make complete sense. There are different types of sentence.

Statement
I was here yesterday.

Question
Where were you yesterday?

Imperative/Order
Be here tomorrow.

Exclamation
You idiot!

Simple sentence

A sentence contains a subject and a verb.

- Charles Dickens wrote *Great Expectations.*

Compound sentence

This is made up of two simple sentences joined by a conjunction.

- Charles Dickens wrote *Great Expectations* and it proved to be an enormous success.

Complex sentence

A **complex sentence** contains one main (independent) clause and at least one subordinate clause. The main clause could stand on its own.

- Charles Dickens, having already established himself as a literary genius, wrote *Great Expectations* in 1861.

Examples
Main clause: Charles Dickens wrote *Great Expectations.*
Subordinate clause: Having already established himself as a literary genius.

A **subordinate clause** cannot stand alone. It is incomplete and needs to be part of a sentence to make sense.

The advantage of simple sentences lies in their clarity. They can be dramatic and effective. Longer sentences are useful when you want to clarify a point or add extra detail.

Do not leave sentences incomplete. The following are examples of incomplete, or unfinished, sentences:

- *As I was watching the match.*
- *Going to school in the rain by bicycle.*
- *If you want to establish your name.*

EXERCISES

Identify the types of sentence in the following list. Are there any incomplete ones?

1. Harold looked at the sky through his binoculars.
2. Anne spent her winters in Dublin, but in summer she went to Cork.
3. Having just finished the exams.
4. I'm totally beat.
5. As the film commenced, he remembered the name of the book.
6. Whether you do it or not.
7. I loved the film because it was so true to life.
8. I believe that there are better actors in Hollywood.
9. Jean, who is Eileen's sister, bought five vinyl records at the market.
10. That's great!

THE PARAGRAPH

Paragraphs are units of writing that help frame ideas and develop points.

Each paragraph should contain one main idea, expressed in a **topic sentence**. Other sentences strengthen and add to the topic sentence. Paragraphs should have a clear aim.

Essays are made up of numerous paragraphs. Each new paragraph begins a new idea or signals a different approach to the subject.

- By dividing your work into paragraphs, you demonstrate that you have structured your work into a logical sequence.
- Remember when depicting dialogue to use a new line for each new speaker.
- In narrative and descriptive writing, paragraphs can be used to change the timeframe or mood of a piece of writing. They are very important for flashback sequences or for suggesting the arrival of a new character.
- The opening and closing paragraphs are usually more effective if kept short.

EXERCISES

1. **Examine the use of paragraphs in the extract below and answer the questions.**

ADVERTISING

We are bombarded with hundreds of advertisements everyday – on the radio and television, in newspapers and magazines, on billboards and in stores. What determines whether we even attend to them, let alone follow their advice?

Consumer psychologists are concerned with the effectiveness of communication between the producers and consumers of goods. Through surveys, as well as in in-depth marketing interviews and tests, psychologists hope to uncover attitudes and feelings towards products as well as unconscious motives for purchasing or not purchasing. They also try to measure what people actually do. Numerous methods include analysis of sales records; actual observations of purchases (by whom, when and where purchases are made); people's ability to identify and distinguish between various brands; and analysis of coupon returns.

An understanding of the purchasing process requires knowledge of three things. It requires knowledge of the consumers – their personality, socioeconomic class, age, sex, ethnic-group membership, buying habits and brand loyalty. Each of these variables affects why, where, with whom and with how much they shop for goods. Then there is the product – its package, which may reflect convenience, security, status, dependability or beauty, its image and its price. Finally, there is the advertising message – the medium it is delivered in, the consumer need it is targeting, whether it is positive (pleasant consequences of product purchase) or negative (unpleasant consequences of product non-purchase).

(The Human Body: The Mind; Into the Inner World)

(a) What is the purpose of the opening paragraph?

(b) Where is the topic sentence in the second paragraph? What do the other sentences do in this paragraph?

(c) Where is the topic sentence in the third paragraph? How does the writer organise his ideas in this paragraph?

(d) From your reading of the above extract, what do you think is the main benefit of writing in paragraphs?

2. Examine the use of paragraphs in the extract below and answer the questions.

BIRTHDAY

On the window sill, a sad snowdrop wilted in its vase. Maggie O'Hara gazed out over the February fields. She was trying to spot the little black lamb that had been born one snowy evening the previous week. Maybe it had been taken in to the warmth of a barn. Maggie was tired standing so she sat in the armchair, waiting for her relatives to make their Sunday visit.

She was trying to remember the last time they were all together. It must have been her husband's funeral. The eight years have gone by too fast. Her family all have busy lives, she thought. Mark, she knew, was busy. That job of his took him all over the country and beyond. He was a great husband and father. Larry was in Australia, settled in well with a wife and three children. Mary never failed her. Every Sunday she appeared for an afternoon chat. Then there was Deirdre. After college, Deirdre took off to London and only made it back for the funeral. Hardly a word since, except for the card at Christmas.

A sharp knock at the door shook Maggie.

"Mrs O'Hara, you have a visitor downstairs," announced Nurse Nolan.

(a) What is the purpose of the opening paragraph?

(b) What does the second paragraph add to our knowledge of the main character?

(c) Why is the third paragraph so short?

(d) Do you think the story has been helped by the use of paragraphs?

The **topic sentence** is the most important sentence in a paragraph.

DRAFTING

A draft is a version of your work that needs to be finished or re-examined. All writers, including professionals such as novelists and journalists, read over their work to check for mistakes and to find ways of improving the expression.

Here is useful checklist of things to look for in a draft version:

DRAFTING CHECKLIST ✓

- Read it aloud – does it flow?
- Can anything be omitted?
- Double check your spelling, punctuation and grammar.
- Look closely at the beginning and end. Are they effective?
- Paragraphs and sentence structure might need amending – are your points clear?
- Is the writing in the correct register? Is it consistent?
- Look out for awkward expression. Make it clear for the reader.
- Needless repetition should be eliminated.
- Vary the verbs and nouns.

GOOD WRITING FLOWS

EXERCISES

Here are four examples of poorly written work that need to be reviewed and partly rewritten. In rewriting them in your copybook, try to preserve the sense of what was intended. You can make as many changes as you think are necessary. Rewrite each, using the following as guidelines:

- Shorten
- Cut out needless repetition
- Strengthen the expression
- Use precise vocabulary
- Punctuate correctly
- Use tenses consistently
- Omit needless adjectives
- Note grammatical/spelling errors

1. The opening of an essay titled: 'Why I like Shakespeare's Hamlet.'

   Shakespeare's *Hamlet* is one of Shakespeare's greatest plays. Hamlet the hero of the play was a brilliant young man who went mad when his father's ghost tells him that his brother murdered him and Hamlet must get revenge by murdering his uncle.

   Throughout the play I really like Hamlet and we the audience want him to do the murder and kill his Uncle, who is called Claudius. The play is exciting especially the way we get to know Hamlet's thoughts by the use of soliloquys. Hamlet is clever, funny, brave but he is also unsure what to do and is a misogynist (hater of women).

2. The opening paragraph of a story set in a city.

   Mandy got home from work in the city of New York and was shocked to find her apartment had been broken into and all her things have been thrown around the apartment. She was going to go to the phone to phone the cops when she noticed something that stopped her in her tracks. Beside the phone was a letter and in a scrawl she read that "We have him". It could only mean one thing. Terri her prize pedigree dog had been stolen for a ransom. Suddenly she had an idea to call her boyfriend. As he is a journalist and so was used to adventures. She got her phone and called Mike that was her boyfriends name.

3. The opening of an essay, 'Why I like Patrick Kavanagh's poetry'.

   Kavanagh for me is my favourite poet. The poems of Kavanagh are interesting because they are not like the poetry of other poets on the course. I can relate to his poetry. He writes on topics such as his relationship with his environment, love and he writes using interesting language. He is my favourite because he has a lot of conflict in his poetry between loving the countryside and hating it. He is also very spiritual and finds peace beside the canal in Dublin especially after his illness.

4. The opening paragraph of an essay on 'Celebrity Culture'.

   In my opinion I think that celebrity culture is overrated. There are far too many people without much talent competing for our attention. There are too many programmes on television like Strictly Come Dancing which contain minor celebrities. If you open the newspapers they are full of news about famous people. Footballers are always seeking attention. It's just ridiculous how they celebrate after scoring a goal. Most celebrities are only famous for a short time before they are forgotten about. I think celebrities are overrated.

HOW CAN I IMPROVE MY WRITING?

Whether you are writing a letter, a review, an essay, a text of a speech or a novel, the most important starting point is to ask yourself the following questions:

- Who am I writing for?
- What do I want to say?
- How do I want to say it?

It is essential to spend time preparing.

Here is a simple step-by-step list to follow:

1. Plan
2. Draft
3. Read
4. Correct
5. Rewrite

You should use a dictionary and thesaurus. These will help to improve your vocabulary. You should also read books, magazines and newspapers. If you are using a thesaurus, remember that not all synonyms have exactly the same meaning.

The following are aspects that you should keep an eye on in your own work. Careful analysis of what you write will reveal mistakes. If you correct these, your writing will improve.

Avoid needless repetition

This is an aspect that can be eliminated by a careful reading of your work. Have a look at these sentences:

> *I really liked the plot of Saving Private Ryan. The plot was interesting from the early scenes. As the plot developed, I found myself totally engrossed from the beginning.*

It is not hard to spot what is wrong with the above lines.

The writer could use *storyline* or *narrative* to make the writing less repetitive. The use of the same word in consecutive sentences should be avoided. As you become a more careful reader of your own work, you will become aware of this problem. The reader is going to notice this and it will affect his/her judgement of your writing.

What about these lines?

> *In the poem, Shakespeare says that he loves his mistress. He also says that time destroys beauty. At the end, he says that he has immortalised his mistresses' beauty in his poem.*

What words can you suggest to this writer to avoid unnecessary repetition?

Choose the right word

Good writers should vary their vocabulary, but you can only do this if you have a wide range of words to choose from.

There are often words that can be used interchangeably, though you should be careful that you substitute an appropriate word and use it in the correct context. Consider these examples:

- see / glimpse / stare / scrutinise / examine
- eat / consume /devour / sample / munch / wolf down
- easy / simple / facile / effortless
- lazy / inactive / indolent / good-for-nothing / slothful
- sleep / slumber / snooze / snore / doze / nap / shuteye / siesta

Each word has a slightly different sense. For instance, think of the sentence "*I see the car*"; it might work as a substitute if you write instead "*I glimpse the car*", but only if that is what you really mean.

Be careful in your deployment of substitute words.

Remember, also, that long and difficult words are not always better than words with which you are comfortable. Simple, clear sentences are generally better than sentences using difficult words that you do not fully understand.

Vary the sentences

It is a good idea to vary the length and structure of sentences. Avoid beginning consecutive sentences with the same words.

Avoid clichés

If you are describing the scene after a snowfall, never refer to a *blanket of snow*. Never write about a morning on which the *birds are singing in the trees*. If someone is hungry, do not write that they could *eat a horse*. These descriptions have become dull and lifeless through overuse.

Of course, you should also avoid the other extreme of using descriptions that are too obscure:

- *It was as dark as the inside of an owl's mouth.*

It is impossible for most readers to relate to this image.

Discard unnecessary words

Do not clutter your writing with words that you can omit. Can you see which of the following words could be discarded?

- *The unmarried bachelor.*
- *The most brilliant boy.*
- *There was this boy in the class.*
- *The economy is severely in deep trouble.*

Effective writing does not need extra words – just the right ones. What about the following examples? Rewrite these sentences in your copybook to make them more effective.

- *Shakespeare's tragedy* Hamlet *is a play concerned with revenge.*
- *The alarm rang at six a.m. in the morning.*
- *In my opinion, I think that* Inception *is a great movie.*
- *I repeated my Leaving Cert and re-sat my exams again.*
- *Irish is a very unique language.*

Do not give offence

Writing is a public act, so do not give offence to (potential) readers. Avoid sexist, racist, homophobic, xenophobic and ageist views. A good writer is able to express strong views without being offensive.

In a similar vein, do not stereotype.

Avoid headings

For the most part, do not use headings. The exception is in some articles or reports where the headings can be a useful structuring device. Never use them in literature essays, personal writing and speeches.

Read aloud

It is essential to read over your written work. Either actually read it aloud, or read it as if it is being said aloud. You will hear what does not sound right. The most important and difficult aspect to get right is the tone. What emotion do you want to be in your work?

A piece of writing works best if there is some variety.

Here is a list of tones and emotions that you might use:

serious	angry	personal
nostalgic	happy	friendly
humorous	sad	impersonal

Presentation

- Neat presentation is a sign of respect to your reader. Ensure that your handwriting is clear.
- Organise your ideas into neat, clearly defined paragraphs.
- The work that you present should be complete and well-structured. Drafting and editing will help you to achieve this.

The best critic of your own work is yourself. Learn to eliminate mistakes.

Notes

SECTION 2

COMPREHENDING A

2

READING A TEXT

Often, we think of **texts** as written material, but a text can be a written, audio or visual construct. The construction of a text determines how we 'read' or understand it.

In this chapter, we will do textual analysis.
We will look at:

- **Why they are written – their purpose.**
- **Who they are aimed at – the audience.**
- **What they are about – their content.**
- **How they are presented – their style.**

We read for a variety of reasons. For example:

- To find out information.
- To be entertained.
- To learn.
- To be convinced of something.
- To be informed.

There are many ways of reading: we might scan the front page of a newspaper; we can scrutinise a poem; we become engrossed in a novel; we carefully read instructions.

When examining any text you are actively:
Reading **Understanding** **Evaluating**

The more interaction you have with a piece of writing, the more rewarding your reading will be. A first reading of a text reveals a number of important factors about its:

- Purpose
- Audience
- Content
- Author
- Style

PURPOSE

Texts are always written for a reason. This might be to:

1. Deliver information
2. Persuade/Argue
3. Tell a story
4. Entertain

1. Delivering Information

Informative texts: Reports, obituaries, articles, travel guides, biographies, autobiographies, photographs, text books, repair manuals, speeches, even diaries, reviews and newspapers all have a clear purpose – to convey information. Such writing contains **facts** and is usually **expressed in a very clear manner**.

The shape and structure of the writing will depend upon the type of information and the purpose in giving it.

2. Persuading and Arguing

Persuasive/argumentative texts: Speeches, newspaper articles, sermons, advertisements, and so on, often have the aim of convincing or persuading their audience. Such texts express opinions, tastes, attitudes, thoughts, preferences and beliefs.

Persuasive writing often makes some **emotional appeal** to the reader. For example, advertisements promote the positive features of a good or service. Newspaper articles might express the writer's opinion on a topic such as drugs in sport or cutbacks in services. The language itself is made appealing through:

- Use of examples and anecdotes.
- Apt comparisons.
- Use of alliteration.
- Words in groups of threes.
- Use of superlatives, e.g. 'most', 'best', 'cleanest'.
- Words with positive connotations.

Argumentative writing is more concerned with facts than opinion. In an argument, there must be **solid support** for viewpoints and assertions. The purpose is to convince the reader by:

- Supporting facts and examples.
- Clear logical structure and consistency.
- Convincing language.
- Use of reason.

Many texts are a mixture of argument and persuasion. Some even include aspects of narrative and descriptive writing.

3. Telling a Story

Narrative texts tell stories. These stories can be based on true events, such as in biography, memoirs, travel writing, diaries, etc., or they can be fictional, as in novels and short stories. The primary purpose of narrative texts is often to **entertain** the reader, but equally important might be the desire to **inform** the reader.

Good narrative writing always sounds true, even when the stories are made up. We look for believable characters, accurate descriptions, realistic dialogue and convincing plots. A writer's success is based on the successful creation of a (sometimes fictional) world. This world can be like ours or totally imaginary. It works when we – the readers – can believe in it.

4. Entertaining

Aesthetic texts use language in a creative way to amuse and entertain the reader. Poetry, short stories and song lyrics fall into this category. Of course, all good writing has an aesthetic element. Where the primary intention cannot be limited to giving information/being persuasive/argumentative/narrative, but is entertaining and fun, we call this **aesthetic**. Much of what we read is for entertainment. We can escape to interesting worlds (such as Hogwarts) and enjoy the contrast with our own more mundane world.

IMPORTANT

In practice, **most texts have more than one purpose**. A powerful, persuasive speech will usually contain information, as well as having entertainment value. A narrative piece of writing can often include information (a historical novel, for example) and aesthetic language.

The above are broad categories to illustrate general points about the intention of a text. However, always remember that texts can have more than one purpose.

AUDIENCE

The **audience** is the group of people for whom a text is written.

A text message, for example, usually has a limited audience. A blog will have a larger audience, but often limited to a group of like-minded readers. A national newspaper's audience is wider again, but can be defined in terms of interests, background, gender, level of education, etc. Sometimes, an audience can be very specific (for example, a film magazine is often limited to those with a particular interest in film), or can be extremely wide (for example, a government brochure dispensing information on a health issue).

An audience may be:

- Specific to age/interest/social grouping.
- General.

CONTENT

The **content** of a text is the information contained in it – its subject matter, the examples, references, and so on.

The content of a book review, for example, might have information about the author, a summary of the plot and something about the setting.

The content of a film poster is composed of a visual, the names of the main actors and director, and some comment about the kind of movie it is.

In a speech, the content can be comprised of facts to support an argument, as well as information that might be important and relevant to the topic.

AUTHOR

The **author** is the writer or composer of a text.

A text always reveals something about its author. The things we learn about an author through our reading of a text include the writer's intention; the writer's attitude to the topic or theme of the text; something of the writer's personality and character. Writers can be objective or subjective. A discerning reader should be aware of a writer's bias.

An author will reveal:

- Intention.
- His/her personality.
- His/her attitudes and opinions.

STYLE

How a text is written – its **style** – is a key aspect in the study of Comprehension. Texts are written differently, depending on the context and the audience for whom they are constructed.

Chapter Three in this book offers a full exploration of style (see page 54).

EXAMINING TEXTS

In the following pages, you can practise and apply what you have learned about **purpose**, **audience**, **content** and the **author**.

How to answer

The questions that follow are designed to find out if your reading of a text has been successful. Before answering, go through the following process:

- Read the question carefully.
- Underline the key word/s in the question.
- Read through the extract, highlighting the appropriate support needed.
- Isolate three or four main points that will be the key to your answer.
- Write an introduction that addresses the question and sets out your approach.
- Use three/four paragraphs to develop the main points in your answer. Have at least one reference/quotation to support each point.
- End with a short conclusion.

TEXT 1

Eileen Battersby travelled out to one of Ireland's most famous historical sites, Skellig Michael, and spent the night on this craggy outcrop. In this article, she writes about her experience. Early Irish monks established a monastery on the inhospitable island in the seventh century. It remained a functioning monastery for 600 years.

This article was originally published in the Irish Times.

A TRIP TO THE SKELLIGS

Part adventure, part odyssey and definite privilege, a visit to Skellig Michael, once an austere Atlantic monastic settlement, now a World Heritage site off the Co. Kerry coast, is a humbling one on several counts.

Some seven or eight sea miles off Valentia, the twin sea crags that are the Skellig rocks come into view and appear to defy any notion of landing. This is no romantic island paradise of shadowy lagoons, freshwater lakes and fruit-bearing trees. There are no trees, and aside from the wonderful birds, heroes in their own right, it looks to be what it is – a twin-peaked plug of rock, content to intrigue rather than welcome.

On climbing the highest ledges of the hazardous South Peak, the views are spectacular. Far below, like a forgotten toy, stands the disused lighthouse. On a breezy late summer's evening of painterly light, the setting is glorious, but it must have been a desolate hell in the bitter wind and rain of a winter storm with wet stone as the only shelter.

Excitement and terror as well a peace and serenity explain the mood of Skellig. Then there is the wonder at the doggedness of the hermit who devised methods of catching and storing rain water, vital on an island with no natural springs or wells and no water supply.

The South Peak's remote hermitage site is far less famous than the image of the monastery itself with its six beehive huts, two boat-shaped oratories built together albeit on varying levels, and inspired location overlooking Little Skellig with the Kerry coastline as a fine backdrop. There are far fewer images of the South Peak and its daring hermitage; visitors are not encouraged to attempt the climb.

Onwards to the monastery itself, on the north of the island. The approach is as dramatic as one could wish, a series of steep stone steps leading ever higher above the sea. For once, I did not regret the absence of the puffins: sweet and docile as they are, their colour dilutes the gravitas of the site. Up the steps, and a view unfolds that is reminiscent of Machu Picchu. Further on up the slope, are more steps and then, on entry through a tunnel in the retaining wall, is the settlement, with its sense of community. The tallest stone cross, the priest's stone, appears to preside over the site, particularly that of the monks' graveyard with its collection of crosses standing erect in a group and appearing to become, as darkness falls, a group of monks looking out over the sea.

Having spent a night on the rock in one of the huts used by Office of Public Works' staff, I was lucky to spy Skellig's most subtle resident, the storm petrel, Europe's smallest sea bird which visits land only while breeding. It hides by day and its one egg is laid in stone walls, often within the monastery complex. One of the beehive huts was serving as nursery to a sturdy Manx shearwater chick. A fluffy, awkward little character, it was trusting enough to be petted. But the storm petrels with their odd purring, cough-like cry are different. Against the absolute blackness of the night sky they were more motion than form.

Sitting in the deserted monastery on a beautiful evening long after the last tourist has left, the final photograph taken, there is a feeling of peace and sadness. The quiet of the beehive cells with their atmosphere of prayer and shelter is both restful and death-like. Every point of the monastery appears to be drawn towards Little Skellig. It is easy to dwell on a friend's remark: "That's a wonderful place, you must empty your mind."

Spiritual and practical, Skellig Michael, its history, its spirit, its silence shattered by the raucous kittiwake, is surrounded by the theatre of the sea and the changing skies. A testament to the art of dry stone masonry, it shimmers in the early morning light once the sea mist disperses. It is a testing self-contained world, not a refuge. It leaves you asking questions. Who were those monks? Why did they come? What made them work so hard and live so dangerously? What devils did they fight? Did they leave Skellig with feelings of sorrow or relief or both? How vast did the sea seem on those dark winter nights?

Before answering the questions, write one-sentence notes in the grid below on the **purpose**, **audience**, **content** and **author** of this **text**.

NOTES

PURPOSE	
AUDIENCE	
CONTENT	
AUTHOR	

EXERCISES

1. What purpose is served by this article? Refer in your answer to the audience that might find it interesting and the writer's intention in writing the article.
2. What kind of person do you think the writer is? Use references to the article to support your answer.
3. The United Nations has awarded World Heritage status to Skellig Michael. What reasons do you think led to this decision?

Here is an extract from a biography of Nora Barnacle, the wife of James Joyce, written by Brenda Maddox. In this extract, we are told of Nora's first meeting with Joyce. According to the biographer, the couple's first date probably took place on 16 June 1904. This date is now celebrated in Dublin as 'Bloomsday', as Joyce chose it for the setting of his most famous novel, Ulysses.

In this passage, a young Galway woman, Nora has made her way to Dublin to work in a hotel.

NORA JOYCE

Nora is remembered as a chambermaid; however, she not only made beds but also waited on tables and, because she was personable and competent, worked at the bar. (It was a duty carrying higher status, for it involved handling money; but the term 'barmaid' would be much used against her in later years.) In every way at Finn's she enjoyed greater independence and companionship than she would have had as a servant in a private house.

Nora was lonely in Dublin, though, and she was not used to loneliness. The city, with its trams, theatres, commuters and floating population, was a metropolis compared to friendly Galway, where she seemed to know everybody. Often her natural good spirits gave way to fits of gloom, and odd aches and pains. Her free time hung heavy. Unless she spoke to strangers she would have had no friends at all except the girls at the hotel.

In Dublin, far more than in Galway, Nora was vulnerable to unwanted male attentions. One of the guests at Finn's, a Mr Holohan, cast lewd eyes upon her and propositioned her.

When a well-mannered, well-spoken, amusing and unthreatening young man [James Joyce] stepped into her path one day in Dublin, therefore, Nora was quite happy to accept his invitation to meet him one evening.

But she did not appear. Joyce took himself to the appointed place at the appointed time and waited until he gave up. A man more sure of himself with women would have gone round to the hotel to find out what had gone wrong. Joyce instead wrote Nora a letter. Its first words, ironically prophetic, convey the haze through which, even at twenty-two, he peered at the world:

> *60 Shelbourne Road*
>
> *June 15, 1904*
>
> *I may be blind. I looked for a long time at a head of reddish-brown hair and decided it was not yours. I went home quite dejected. I would like to make an appointment but it might not suit you. I hope you will be kind enough to make one with me – if you have not forgotten me!*
>
> *James A. Joyce.*

Nora had not forgotten him. Most probably she failed to keep the rendezvous because she could not get the evening off and had no way of letting him know. Once she had received his letter with his address, however, she was able to accept his second invitation and that time did not disappoint him.

Was the day of their first date, Thursday June 16, 1904? Probably. That is the best that can be said. There is no evidence from letters or diaries that June 16 was the day that divided the lives of Nora Barnacle and James Joyce into before and after – none, apart from the date of the action of *Ulysses*.

Before answering the questions, write one-sentence notes in the grid below on the **purpose**, **audience**, **content** and **author** of this **text**.

NOTES

PURPOSE	
AUDIENCE	
CONTENT	
AUTHOR	

EXERCISES

1. What are the most important facts that we learn from this extract?
2. What evidence is there that the author has researched her subject?
3. What do we learn about Nora Barnacle and James Joyce from this extract?
4. Who do you think might be interested in reading this biography of Nora Barnacle?

TEXT 3

This extract is taken from an article written by former Mayor of New York Ed Koch. In the article, Koch outlines his reasons for supporting the death penalty.

THE CASE FOR CAPITAL PUNISHMENT

Because I support the death penalty for heinous crimes of murder, I have sometimes been the subject of emotional and outraged attacks by voters who find my position reprehensible or worse. I have listened to their ideas. I have weighed their objections carefully. I still support the death penalty. The reasons I maintain my position can be best understood by examining the arguments most frequently heard in opposition.

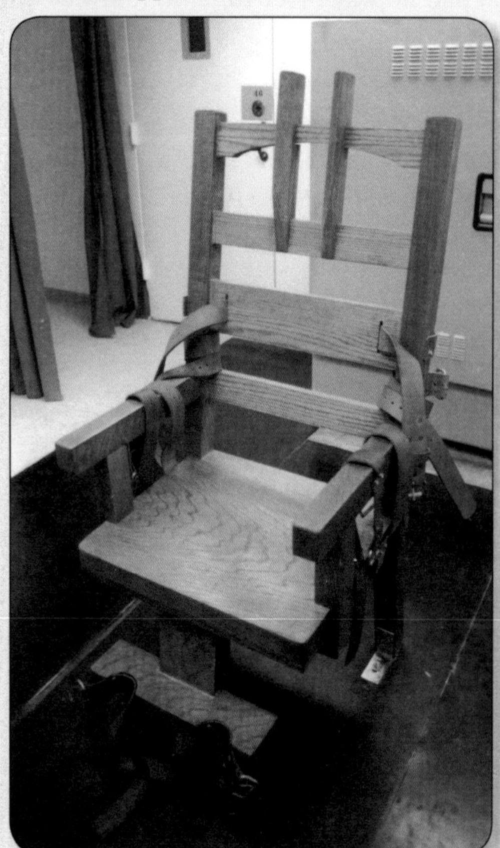

1. The death penalty is 'barbaric'.

Sometimes, opponents of capital punishment horrify with tales of lingering death on the gallows, of faulty electric chairs, or of agony in the gas chamber. Partly in response to such protests, several states such as North Carolina and Texas switched to execution by lethal injection. The condemned person is put to death painlessly, without ropes, voltage, bullets, or gas. Did this answer the objections of death penalty opponents? Of course not. On June 22, 1984, the *New York Times* published an editorial that sarcastically attacked the new 'hygienic' method of death by injection, and stated that "execution can never be made humane through science." So it's not the method that really troubles opponents. It's the death itself they consider barbaric.

2. No other major democracy uses the death penalty.

No other major democracy – in fact, few other countries of any description – is plagued by a murder rate such as that in the United States. Fewer and fewer Americans can remember the days when unlocked doors were the norm and murder was a rare and terrible offence. In America the murder rate climbed 122 per cent between 1953 and 1980. During that same period, the murder rate in New York City increased by almost 400 per cent, and the statistics are even worse in many other cities. A study at MIT showed that based on 1970 homicide rates a person who lived in a large American city ran a greater risk of being murdered than an American soldier in World War II ran of being killed in combat. It is not surprising that the laws of each country differ according to differing conditions and traditions. If other countries had our murder problem, the cry for capital punishment would be just as loud as it is here. And I dare say that any other major democracy where 75 per cent of people supported the death penalty would soon enact it into law.

3. An innocent person might be executed by mistake.

Consider the work of Hugo Adam Bedau, one of the most implacable foes of capital punishment in this country. According to Mr Bedau, it is "false sentimentality to argue that the death penalty should be abolished because of the abstract possibility that an innocent person might be executed." He cites a study of the 7,000 executions in this country from 1893 to 1971, and concludes that the record fails to show that such cases occur. The main point, however, is this. If government functioned only when the possibility of error didn't exist, government wouldn't function at all. Human life deserves special protection, and one of the best ways to guarantee that protection is to assure that convicted murderers do not kill again. Only the death penalty can accomplish this end. In a recent case in New Jersey, a man named Richard Biegenwald was freed from prison after serving 18 years for murder; since his release he has been convicted of committing four murders. A prisoner named Lemuel Smith, who while serving four life sentences for murder (plus two life sentences for kidnapping and robbery) in New York's Green Haven Prison, lured a woman corrections officer into the chaplain's office and strangled her. He then mutilated and dismembered her body. An additional life sentence for Smith is meaningless. Because New York has no death penalty statute, Smith has effectively been given a licence to kill.

4. Capital punishment cheapens the value of human life.

On the contrary, it can be easily demonstrated that the death penalty strengthens the value of human life. If the penalty for rape were lowered, clearly it would signal a lessened regard for the victims' suffering, humiliation and personal integrity. It would cheapen their horrible experience and expose them to an increased danger or recurrence. When we lower the penalty for murder, it signals a lessened regard for the value of the victim's life. Some critics of capital punishment, such as columnist Jimmy Breslin, have suggested that a life sentence is actually a harsher penalty for murder than death. This is sophistic nonsense. A few killers may decide not to appeal a death sentence, but the overwhelming majority make every effort to stay alive. It is by exacting the highest penalty for the taking of human life that we affirm the highest value of human life.

5. Thou Shalt Not Kill

The Bible is our greatest source of moral inspiration. Opponents of the death penalty frequently cite the sixth of the Ten Commandments in an attempt to prove that capital punishment is divinely proscribed. In the original Hebrew, however, the Sixth Commandment reads, "Thou Shalt Not Commit Murder," and the Torah specifies capital punishment for a variety of offences. The biblical viewpoint has been upheld by philosophers throughout history. The greatest thinkers of the 19th century – Kant, Locke, Hobbes, Rousseau, Montesquieu and Mill – agreed that natural law properly authorises the sovereign to take life in order to vindicate justice.

The United States Constitution, widely admired as one of the seminal achievements in the history of humanity, condemns cruel and inhuman punishment, but does not condemn capital punishment.

Before answering the questions, write one-sentence notes in the grid below on the **purpose**, **audience**, **content** and **author** of this **text**.

NOTES

PURPOSE	
AUDIENCE	
CONTENT	
AUTHOR	

EXERCISES

1. What is the main argument that the writer presents to us? Give reasons for your answer.
2. How does the writer's use of information help to advance his argument? You must give reasons for your answer.
3. How would you describe the tone and language used in this essay? Illustrate with reference to the article.
4. How would you describe the writer? Is he fair/biased/neutral/intelligent/passionate? You must support your answer.

TEXT 4

This article on alcohol by Mary Kenny appeared in the Irish Independent *following the inquest into the death of popular singer Amy Winehouse.*

'CIGARETTES ARE NOTHING LIKE AS HARMFUL AS ALCOHOL'

Young people lose their lives in tragic circumstances every day, and too often I am reminded of those lines from Tennyson which my mother would sadly quote: "Never morning wore to evening/But some heart did break."

But the death of Amy Winehouse had a wider reach, as it may emblemise a wider tragedy – the harm done by alcohol and alcoholism to young people.

We are, by now, aware of the dangers of illegal drugs such as heroin, cocaine and even marijuana (which research has shown can be a trigger for schizophrenia).

We are constantly told how evil cigarettes are, and Health Minister James Reilly has ever-more draconian plans to restrict their sale and to place ever-more horrendous images of death and disease on cigarette packets.

But cigarettes are nothing like as harmful as the legal drug of alcohol. Cigarettes can contribute to heart disease and a range of cancers, but nobody gets into a motor car, drives at 100mph and kills himself and four other people because he's smoked a packet of ciggies. Nobody goes home and beats up their spouse and children senseless because they've had one too many Silk Cut. Amy was not found dead in bed at the age of 27 – a glittering career ahead of her, and a fabulous range of achievements behind her – because she overdosed on Marlboro.

Even if she had been smoking four packets of cigarettes a day, it would have taken, on average, a further three decades for the habit to prove a fatal one.

Why do we have a culture which penalises someone in the catering trade up to €5,000 for allowing a cigarette to be smoked on the premises, but tolerates every kind of light-hearted drollerie about getting pissed, plastered, sloshed, canned, and out of it?

I'm not just talking of Ireland. Last year, I went to buy an 18th birthday card for a young English cousin, and guess what was on every available birthday card for 18-year-olds? Jubilatory congratulations for the chance to get sizzled out of your head. It took me ages to find a birthday card for an 18-year-old which didn't have carousing illustrations of inebriation.

We don't send cards to 18-year-olds with glorious pictures of tobacco, although a cigarette would take a lot longer to damage their health than a drink habit.

We don't stigmatise drinkers, either, in the way we stigmatise smokers. We don't tell boozers that if they must have a swig, could they do so in the back garden?

All right, smoke smells in a way that vodka doesn't – vodka, in particular, is odourless, which is why alcoholics favour it, as Amy did. But are we talking about health and death, or good house-keeping?

I won't be hypocritical about this: in my misspent youth, I drank for Ireland and could well have met the same fate as Amy Winehouse. In Kinsale, the poet Derek Mahon once probably saved my life, and possibly the lives of others, by physically restraining me from drunkenly driving a car back to my lodgings.

There certainly is an argument for authoritarian intervention when someone is about to do something self-destructive to themselves and potentially harmful to others. But I've had time, now, to reflect on the hows and the whys of alcohol abuse, and I've seen the terrible cost paid by individuals and families when alcoholism takes hold.

And, in contrast to the medical mania about banning cigarettes, it seems to me that the medical profession doesn't take alcoholism half seriously enough. An alcoholic showing up in a GP's surgery is given a few anti-depressant pills – that is, go off and replace one drug with another – and told to consider counselling or self-help groups. Could this be because doctors, nowadays, don't often smoke but they may be liberal imbibers of alcohol themselves?

I have reflected a lot on the way we were educated about alcohol when I was growing up, and whether this helped or hindered. Too much finger-wagging against the dangers of drink can be counter-productive (too much moralising about anything elicits a natural rebellion). After all, Amy Winehouse came from an orthodox Jewish background, and Jewish tradition deeply disapproved of heavy drinkers. Alcoholism is almost unknown among religious Jews. Yet, evidently, individuals can slip through the net.

You can't forbid too much, or coerce youngsters into taking the pledge, as whole generations in Ireland were made to do. I went from an Ireland where teenagers did not drink to a France where wine was as natural as water and manual workers began their morning shift with "le petit pot" of Calvados. The swing from prohibition to permissiveness was the gateway to temptation. Right through my 20s, I thought anyone who didn't drink copiously was stuffy. But I've wept bitter tears since.

We don't have to be prohibitionist, or stuffy, about liquor, but surely the death of Amy Winehouse – she was more than five times over the drink-driving limit when she drew her last – should help to diminish the acceptance that getting sloshed out of your head is amusing, and having a killer hangover is a sign of a great night out.

Shouldn't we be mindful of Shakespeare's words in Othello: "That men should put an enemy in their mouths to steal away their brains!"

Or in poor Amy's case, to steal away her life.

Before answering the questions, write one-sentence notes in the grid below on the **purpose**, **audience**, **content** and **author** of this **text**.

NOTES

PURPOSE	
AUDIENCE	
CONTENT	
AUTHOR	

EXERCISES

1. "Cigarettes are nothing like as harmful as alcohol." Does the writer convince you that this statement is true? Refer in your answer to the extract.
2. What do you learn about the author? Support with reference to the text.
3. Is this a suitable article for a national newspaper to publish? In your answer, refer to its purpose and the effect it might have on its readership.
4. Comment on what you liked, or did not like, about the way this article has been written. Use examples to support your views.

TEXT 5

The novel Frankenstein *was written by Mary Shelley in the summer of 1816. A group of friends were staying in a villa in France. A thunderstorm made it impossible to go out for days. The friends had a bet to see who could write the scariest novel. One of the results was this famous story.*

In the novel, Doctor Frankenstein has been experimenting on corpses, trying to find a way of bringing them back to life. In the following adapted extract, he is shocked by his own success. The English is a little old-fashioned.

FRANKENSTEIN

Winter, spring and summer passed away during my labours; but I did not watch the blossom or the expanding leaves – sights which before always yielded me supreme delight – so deeply was I engrossed in my occupation. The leaves of that year had withered before my work drew near to a close; and now every day showed more plainly how I had succeeded. But my enthusiasm was checked by my anxiety, and I appeared rather like one doomed by slavery to toil in the mines, or any other unwholesome trade, than an artist occupied by his favourite employment. Every night I was oppressed by a slow fever, and I became nervous to a most painful degree; the fall of a leaf startled me, and I shunned my fellow-creatures as if I had been guilty of a crime. Sometimes I grew alarmed at the wreck I perceived that I had become; the energy of my purpose alone sustained me: my labours would soon end, and I believed that exercise and amusement would then drive away incipient disease; and I promised myself both of these when my creation should be complete.

It was on a dreary night of November that I beheld the result of all my work. It was already one in the morning; the rain pattered dismally against the panes, and my candle was nearly burnt out, when, by the glimmer of the half-extinguished light, I saw the dull yellow eye of the creature open; it breathed hard, and a movement agitated its limbs.

How can I describe my shock at seeing the wretch whom I had worked so hard to create? His limbs were in proportion, and I had chosen features for him I had thought beautiful. Beautiful! Great God! His yellow skin scarcely covered the mass of muscles and arteries beneath; his hair was of a lustrous black, and flowing; his teeth of a pearly whiteness. These aspects formed a more horrid contrast with his watery eyes, that seemed almost of the same colour as the colourless sockets in which they were set, his shrivelled complexion and straight black lips.

I had worked hard for nearly two years, for the sole purpose of putting life into a dead body. For this I had deprived myself of rest and health. I had desired it more than anything; but now that I had finished, the beauty of the dream vanished, and breathless horror and disgust filled my heart. Unable to endure the sight of the being I had created, I rushed out of the room.

For a long time I remained in my bedchamber, walking up and down, unable to sleep. At length tiredness overcame me and I threw myself on the bed in my clothes, seeking a few moments of forgetfulness. But it was disturbed by the wildest dreams. I thought I saw my beloved, Elizabeth, in the bloom of health, walking in the streets of Ingolstadt. Delighted and surprised, I embraced her; but as I imprinted the first kiss on her lips, they turned the colour of death. Her features appeared to change, and I thought that I held the corpse of my dead mother in my arms; a shroud covered her and I saw the grave-worms crawling in the folds of the cloth. I jumped from my sleep in horror; a cold dew covered my forehead, my teeth chattered, and every limb shook. Suddenly I saw the creature by the dim and yellow light of the moon, as it forced its way through the window shutters. He held up the curtain, and stared at me. His jaws opened, and he muttered some inarticulate sounds, while a grin wrinkled his cheeks. He might have spoken, but I did not hear; one hand was stretched out, seemingly to detain me, but I escaped, and rushed down stairs.

Oh! No mortal could bear the horror of that sight. An Egyptian mummy brought back to life could not be so hideous as that wretch.

Before answering the questions, write one-sentence notes in the grid below on the **purpose**, **audience**, **content** and **author** of this **text**.

NOTES

PURPOSE	
AUDIENCE	
CONTENT	
AUTHOR	

EXERCISES

1. "The purpose of this novel is to teach as much as to scare." Respond to this statement. Use the text to support your answer.
2. What do you learn about the character of Doctor Frankenstein from the extract? Support your answer.
3. Which of the paragraphs would make the best material for a scene in a film of *Frankenstein*? Give reasons for your answer.

Read this passage taken from a book called the Xenophobe's Guide to Ireland. *The author, Frank McNally, takes a humorous approach to the task of explaining Ireland to those not familiar with the subject. This is from the opening section called 'Nationalism and Identity'.*

A XENOPHOBE'S GUIDE TO IRELAND

There is a country called Ireland and a state called Ireland, and these are not the same thing. The country called Ireland includes Northern Ireland whereas the state called Ireland once claimed to include it, and now merely aspires to include it, eventually. For the moment, a majority of Northern Ireland's population prefers the status quo (union* with Great Britain, that is, not the 1970s rock band).

You may know Ireland as "The Republic of Ireland", but this is only a working title. The name of the state is "Ireland", or in the Irish language "Eire". For obvious reasons, the pro-British majority of Northern Ireland dislikes using the term "Ireland" to refer to the Republic. So although they have no enthusiasm for the Irish language, they often use the term "Eire" in English. This is considered an insult by the people in the Republic, and is intended as such by Northern Ireland unionists, although both sides would have a hard job to explain why. English people sometimes use "Eire" without intended insult, which is OK because they don't know any better.

Many people in the Republic don't like using the term Northern Ireland, because the capital letters make it look too permanent. Depending on how nationalistic they are, they prefer to call it "the occupied six counties" (extreme nationalist), "the wee six" (extreme nationalist with folksy sense of humour), "the north of Ireland" (moderate nationalist), or just "the North", complete with capital N (liberal, sophisticated, hardly nationalist at all, just making a point). Pro-British northerners also sometimes use the province-name "Ulster" for Northern Ireland. But Northern Ireland contains only two-thirds of Ulster – the rest is in the Republic, and people there don't like the U-name being misappropriated.

In short, the country called Ireland is a diplomatic minefield for the unwary. The safest thing is to refer informally to "the north" and "the south". If you speak fast enough, no-one will be able to tell whether you're using capital letters. Just remember that the most northerly part of the south – Donegal – is further north than anywhere in the north. Otherwise, the already high risk of getting lost in Ireland (see Road Signs) will be increased unnecessarily.

*which is why they are called Unionists

Before answering the questions, write one-sentence notes in the grid below on the **purpose**, **audience**, **content** and **author** of this **text**.

NOTES

PURPOSE	
AUDIENCE	
CONTENT	
AUTHOR	

EXERCISES

1. What is the purpose of this extract? Give reasons for your answer.
2. In what kind of book/magazine might you find this extract? Consider the tone of the writing in your answer, as well as the content.
3. What kind of person do you consider the writer to be? Give reasons.

TEXT 7

This article on the genre of science fiction begins with two definitions before discussing the topic itself.

DEFINING SCIENCE FICTION

1. **Robert A. Heinlein**: "A handy short definition of almost all science fiction might read: realistic speculation about possible future events, based solidly on adequate knowledge of the real world, past and present, and on a thorough understanding of the nature and significance of the scientific method."
2. **Rod Serling**: "Science fiction is the improbable made possible, and fantasy is the impossible made probable."

Since ancient times, man has wondered how to create perfection here on earth. Plato's Republic, from the fifth century BC, offers a description of the perfect state; one ruled by an aristocracy who have been educated in the art of government. It is a society ruled by the highest principles of wisdom. Plato rejects both democracy and poets, seeing no place for either in his perfect Republic – both (according to Plato) are too concerned with the pursuit of short-term pleasure and beauty rather the attainment of moral and philosophical truth and goodness.

Though Plato's work cannot be considered a work of science fiction, it does raise concerns similar to the ones that occupy the minds of science fiction writers. What is the perfect society? How can happiness be guaranteed? Are individual freedom and social harmony compatible? Is man's nature determined by nature or nurture?

Classics such as Jonathan Swift's *Gulliver's Travels* and Thomas Moore's *Utopia* describe imaginary lands that are blueprints for utopian and/or dystopian societies. In both cases the writers' primary concern seems to be to get the reader to ask questions about how we live our lives and how we want to live our lives. Both writers are moralists who use their work to satirise and lampoon human behaviour and political systems.

Since the onset of the Industrial Revolution, technology has changed the lives of humans, and this change has accelerated exponentially in the last hundred years or so. Faced with this, writers have been confronted with having to imagine societies not at a huge remove from our own but some years in the future. Science has changed our world and many writers confront these changes in a genre we know as science fiction. What will this future be like? Such speculation has given us wonderful novels such as Orwell's *1984*, Huxley's *Brave New World*; Arthur C Clarke's *2001: A Space Odyssey.* Science Fiction is one of the most popular genres of this era. It seems to have captured our deepest anxieties about the future and our most optimistic projections. We see change happening all around us and it is natural that we should ask if this is going to lead to our salvation or destruction.

Take the example of communication in the very recent past. From the humble letter, through a succession of incredible and profoundly life-changing inventions, including the telegram, telephone, mobile phone, and the Internet, communication between humans has altered the way we live our lives. These changes affect our relationships with one another, how we organize society, and our relationship with our planet. An optimist sees these changes as essentially good, each new invention making our lives easier, giving us mastery over our environment. The pessimist, however, questions this and sees flaws in the way technology is used (and will continue to be used). The political, religious, social and cultural aspects of a future dominated increasingly by technology demands thought and imagination. This is where our great science fiction writers come in. The more hopeful imagine the creation of a perfect society, but others offer a darker vision and speculate on a future in which we might become, not masters of technology, but mastered by it.

Some science fiction writers of the past have offered us remarkably accurate glimpses of the future (which is our present). Space travel, television, in-vitro fertilisation, robots, sliding doors, kindle books, video-phones have all appeared in novels before been actually invented. This begs the question: will time travel become a reality? Will flying cars be invented? Will we find ways of communicating telepathetically? Will we conquer the ageing process? Or will each invention not simply test our humanity thereby confronting us with new problems that we must solve?

The appeal of science fiction is that it combines scientific knowledge with an artist's imagination. Throw in a philosophical and ethical dimension, and you have the recipe for truly engrossing work.

Before answering the questions, write one-sentence notes in the grid below on the **purpose**, **audience**, **content** and **author** of this **text**.

NOTES

PURPOSE	
AUDIENCE	
CONTENT	
AUTHOR	

EXERCISES

1. State as clearly as you can the purpose of this article.
2. Do you think this article has been written for the general reader or a more specific readership? Give reasons for your answer.
3. From reading this article, do you think that science fiction can be an 'engrossing' genre? Support your answer with reference to the text.

This poem by Rudyard Kipling is often quoted. Though written over 100 years ago, its appeal has endured. Read it carefully before answering.

IF

If you can keep your head when all about you
Are losing theirs and blaming it on you;
If you can trust yourself when all men doubt you,
But make allowance for their doubting too:
If you can wait and not be tired by waiting,
Or, being lied about, don't deal in lies,
Or being hated don't give way to hating,
And yet don't look too good, nor talk too wise;

If you can dream – and not make dreams your master;
If you can think – and not make thoughts your aim,
If you can meet with Triumph and Disaster
And treat those two impostors just the same:
If you can bear to hear the truth you've spoken
Twisted by knaves to make a trap for fools,
Or watch the things you gave your life to, broken,
And stoop and build'em up with worn-out tools;

If you can make one heap of all your winnings
And risk it on one turn of pitch-and-toss,
And lose, and start again at your beginnings,
And never breathe a word about your loss:
If you can force your heart and nerve and sinew
To serve your turn long after they are gone,
And so hold on when there is nothing in you
Except the Will which says to them: "Hold on!"

If you can talk with crowds and keep your virtue,
Or walk with Kings – nor lose the common touch,
If neither foes nor loving friends can hurt you,
If all men count with you, but none too much:
If you can fill the unforgiving minute
With sixty seconds' worth of distance run,
Yours is the Earth and everything that's in it,
And – which is more – you'll be a Man, my son!

Before answering the questions, write one-sentence notes in the grid below on the **purpose**, **audience**, **content** and **author** of this **text**.

NOTES

PURPOSE	
AUDIENCE	
CONTENT	
AUTHOR	

EXERCISES

1. Why do you think this poem has remained so popular? Give reasons based on your reading of the poem.
2. This poem has often been displayed as a poster. Suggest a place that you might like to display it as a poster. Give reasons for your choice.
3. What is the most valuable piece of advice that is offered in the poem? Give reasons for your choice.

REMEMBER

When you read a comprehension passage, consider:
• AUTHOR • AUDIENCE • CONTENT • STYLE • PURPOSE
Then **READ, COMPREHEND, EVALUATE, INTERPRET** AND **RESPOND**!

STRUCTURE YOUR ANSWER

You must always remember to coherently structure your written work.
In general, an answer should be divided as follows:

- **INTRODUCTION** – address question/frame response
- **MAIN BODY** – 3 or 4 main points with support and comments
- **CONCLUSION**

Notes

STYLE

INTRODUCTION

Style refers to how a text is written. How a comprehension passage is written is as important as its content. This chapter helps you to examine and understand the style that a writer uses. A writer's originality and success is rooted in the style of writing.

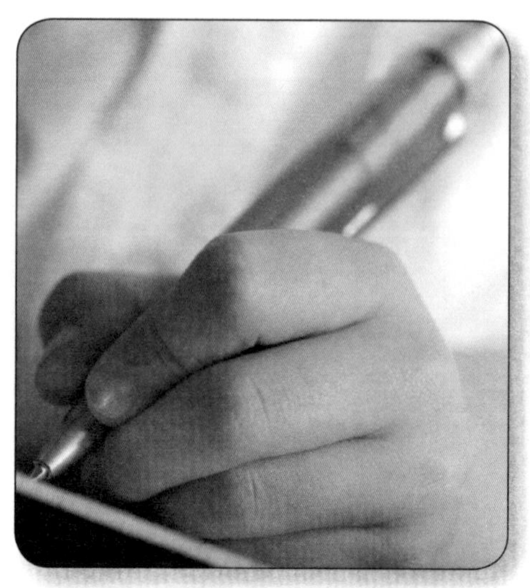

The style of writing should:

- **Reinforce a writer's purpose.**
- **Be appropriate to the task.**
- **Connect with the audience.**
- **Complement the content.**
- **Make the reading interesting.**

The following is a helpful glossary of stylistic features that you will come across in comprehension exercises. You will also learn to use these features yourself when you do functional writing exercises and write compositions.

GLOSSARY OF KEY TERMS

ALLITERATIVE PHRASING – Can be used for emphasis, to create a pleasant rhythm in the writing: *The wonderful winter snow made daytime delightful.* In descriptive writing, it can be used occasionally for onomatopoeic effect: *The fire crackled and soon the building crashed to the ground.*

In persuasive language, it adds to the emotional appeal of the writing, thereby highlighting a point, e.g. *Prison penalises the poor.*

Newspaper headlines often use alliteration to attract readers, e.g. *Cops Catch Cold Killer.*

The tone of a text is often affected by alliteration.

ALLUSION – A reference to a well-known historical, mythological, religious individual or event. The use of allusion gives substance to a point, e.g. *The story of Midas has much that might be relevant in our country today.*

ANECDOTES – These are brief stories of an informal nature that are used to illustrate a point. Often employed in speeches and sermons. In persuasive writing, they can help to support a point or develop an argument, e.g. *When I was young I was deeply disturbed by my first encounter with a jellyfish. I remember it was a particularly hot day.*

AUDIENCE – This refers to the readers of a text. Writers adapt their writing to suit the audience. The audience of a newspaper article on the topic of global warming is obviously a different one to the audience of a speech given to a group of First Year secondary school pupils. The register is a crucial aspect, as well as the structure and layout.

CLICHÉ – An overused phrase or comparison. Clichés are best avoided ("like the plague"), but can add humour if used knowingly, e.g. *Footballers who give 110% are often over the moon if they get a result.*

Politicians, sportsmen and journalists are the worst offenders.

It is best to avoid descriptions that have lost their punch through over-use, e.g. *a blanket of snow*, or *the sun was cracking the stones*.

COLLOQUIAL LANGUAGE – Words and expressions that are used in everyday life but considered too informal for most kinds of written expression. Writers, however, often use colloquial expression to give their writing a sense of reality (verisimilitude).

- "I ain't doing nothing!"
- "Am I bovered? Do I look bovered?"
- "Leinster rugby is like the best ever, right."

Slang is closely related. In slang, old words can be given new meanings or new words invented. Many groups within society invent their own slang (e.g. Cockney rhyming slang, schoolboy/girl slang). Slang terminology is inventive and always changing. Sometimes, it is offensive and is best avoided in polite conversation. Do the following words mean anything to you beyond the literal meaning?

- *Dude*
- *Heino*
- *Bog*
- *Bread*

DICTION and **VOCABULARY** – These are the words a writer uses. The words should be appropriate to the subject. There are many words for money but they are not all the same in meaning. Pay attention also to the use of verbs, adjectives and imagery in a text.

Effective writing is made so because of the quality of the words chosen. In persuasive writing, the writer is trying to convince us of an opinion. You will notice how the words help in doing this. Likewise, a descriptive piece will contain plenty of adjectives and imagery.

DIDACTIC – This is used to describe the tone of a piece of writing that sets out to teach.

EUPHEMISMS – Polite expressions that are indirect in expressing an idea, e.g. *I am going to powder my nose,* and *The soldier died in friendly fire.*

EXAGGERATION / HYPERBOLE – To emphasise a point for purposes of comparison/humour, e.g. *Football is not a matter of life and death. It is much more important than that,* or *I am not saying the band was bad, but four lobotomised sloths on valium could entertain an audience better.*

EXAMPLES – Used to flesh out points, illustrate ideas. In persuasive and argumentative writing, examples are needed in giving support and weight to one's views.

Example:

> *Studies in the U.S. have demonstrated that capital punishment is no deterrent to murderers. States such as Texas which execute prisoners do not have lower incidences of murder. We can also point to the high murder rate in Victorian England when hanging was a daily occurrence.*

IMAGERY – Very effective in creating a visual picture or for clarifying a point. Good images can be witty and clever in a personal essay. They add to the entertainment value of a piece of work. In descriptive writing, imagery is essential in helping us to imagine a scene or for creative mood or atmosphere.

SIMILE – This is a comparison that uses 'like' or 'as'. For example, Ernest Hemingway describes a café as *like a battleship stripped for action*. The best similes are original. Avoid cliched similes such like *as sick as a parrot*, or *like a bull in a china shop*. These are stale and add little to a description. Moreover, if similes are too vague, they will not be understood, e.g. *He ate as much as a camel in heat*. What does this mean? Is it a lot or very little?

METAPHOR –Metaphors are comparisons that do not use 'like' or 'as', e.g. *The festival exploded*.

PERSONIFICATION – This is when human qualities are given to non-human entities, e.g. *The city slept; the sun watched over us; the trees whistled in the breeze*.

LISTING – A good way for a writer to emphasise or convey an idea is by producing a list of examples. Describing the rain that fell during his Limerick childhood, Frank McCourt wrote:

> *It created a cacophony of hacking coughs, bronchial rattles, asthmatic wheezes, consumptive croaks. It turned noses into fountains, lungs into bacterial sponges. It provoked cures galore; to ease the catarrh you boiled onions in milk blackened with pepper; for the congested passages you made a paste of boiled flour and nettle, wrapped it in a rag, and slapped it, sizzling on the chest.*

Lists can be used effectively in both persuasive and narrative writing.

MOOD – The atmosphere that is created by a piece of writing. Here a sombre mood is created:

> *The beach was deserted and dark clouds approached from far out at sea. Even the gulls had disappeared, leaving only the sound of breakers against the shingles.*

QUOTATION and **REFERENCE** – The use of quotations from famous writers or figures of authority give substance to an argument. The Bible and Shakespeare are quoted by many writers. The use of quotations gives weight to an argument.

If only we as a nation had taken the advice that Polonius gave to his son Laertes: *Neither a borrower nor a lender be*.

PARTICIPLES – The present participle is that form of a verb that ends in 'ing'. Participles can act like an adjective and can give energy to a description, e.g. *The growing, surging and threatening crowd approached the police line*.

PURPOSE – There are many reasons why a text has been written. The most common purposes are:

- To give information
- To persuade
- To tell a story
- To describe
- To motivate
- To please/entertain

The purpose will determine the way a text is written.

REGISTER – The range of words and expressions we can choose from. We choose language appropriate to our task, depending on our purpose and audience.

FORMAL REGISTER – This is the most polite and common expression used in newspapers and articles. It tends to be quite formal. Such writing is clear and concise. This is the language used in editorials, reports and obituaries. It is also the language you would use when addressing your principal!

INFORMAL REGISTER – The language we use when communicating with those we know, or can relax with. Read this list of people and match the likely salutations:

bishop	dude
judge	Your Grace
surfing friend	Your Honour
bank manager	Sir
school principal	honey
husband	Mr Ryan

Change them around and see how foolish they might sound!

The informal register includes colloquial language and slang.

RHETORICAL LANGUAGE – We use this to emphasise a point. It is associated with the tone of voice in debating. Typical devices are:

- **The rhetorical question**, e.g. *Can we expect the little man to pay the price of our banks' foolishness?*

- **Repetition**. Remember Barack Obama's use of the phrase "Yes we can!"

Note: Not all questions are rhetorical!

SOUND – We often associate alliteration, assonance, sibilance and onomatopoeia with poetry, but these devices can be used in persuasive and narrative writing. They add to the appeal of the writing and help convey a mood.

- *Fortune favours the brave.*
- *The soft moonlight shone on the surface of the sea.*
- *Maria crashed and banged saucepans in her attempt to get dinner ready on time.*

SUPERLATIVES – The highest degree of comparison of the quality of an adjective or adverb. This is usually indicated by 'most'. Examples are highest, fastest, biggest, best, most efficient, etc. Superlatives are an efficient tool in persuasive writing. Advertisers use them excessively.

TEXT – This refers to any written or visual or audio work. Prayers, poems, novels, articles, speeches, films, photographs, advertisements are all examples of texts. We study texts in terms of:

- *Language*
- *Purpose*
- *Audience*
- *Register*
- *Tone*
- *Structure*
- *Layout*

TONE – The attitude of a writer to a subject. It can be clear if a writer is angry, happy, ironic.

- *August 5th, 2010 lives on in my memory like a scene from a favourite movie. I can replay every moment: the candlelit dinner, the packed club that seemed to contain just us two and a kiss as I left her to her door.*
- *I propose a new tax to enable our top bankers to live the cosy lifestyles they so deserve.*
- *Football is being destroyed by greedy clubs, dishonest players and unsporting fans.*

TRIADIC PHRASING – The structuring of words, phrases and sentences in groups of three. Very effective in persuasive writing.

- *Eat, drink and be merry!*
- *We must remember to bring pens, copies and books.*
- *The pleasure of the summer months lies in being able to eat outdoors, having over 12 hours of sunshine and seeing the halo of happiness that the sun brings to people.*

REPETITION – This is used for the purposes of emphasis.

- *The fools, the fools, the fools.*

RHETORICAL QUESTION – The person asking the question does not really expect an answer when a rhetorical question is asked. It is used for emphasis and getting a point across.

- *Do you really think I am buying that excuse?*
- *Is it fair to expect the poorest and most vulnerable to have to pay for health services?*
- *You expect me to believe that you're late because a lightning bolt struck and damaged only your alarm clock?*

It is important to note that narrative/persuasive/informative and descriptive writing will each have their own unique styles.

NOTE: For example, in a persuasive text, we can expect examples, rhetorical devices and a convincing tone. In a descriptive text, there will be an emphasis on imagery and use of verbs and adjectives.

PARAGRAPHS – Units of writing that help a writer to organise and develop a point and help the reader to follow the point. Although there is no strict law governing when to use paragraphs, it is accepted that when a new idea is introduced you will go on to a new paragraph. Good paragraph formation comes with practice.

Paragraphs should be examined to ascertain:

- How ideas are developed.
- How mood is established.

- How a logical argument is developed.

SENTENCES – The most important sentence in any piece of work is the **topic sentence**. This gives the gist of the entire paragraph. Topic sentences are usually placed at the beginning of a paragraph, but sometimes they are held back to the end for dramatic effect.

Short sentences can be highly effective in a number of ways. A few of them in a paragraph can create suspense as they interrupt the natural rhythm. They can be dramatic.

She opened the door. A sharp noise alerted her. She crept to the foot of the stairs. A light was shining under the door of the main bedroom. She could hear a scraping sound.

They can also be used to gather a number of disjointed thoughts, as in this example from a diary:

3rd March: Tomorrow find out what film the expression "Are you talking to me?" comes from. Get the video fixed. Ring Jane and apologise for the scene in the cafeteria. Oh, and begin studying. Just three months to go.

Used like this they can help establish character.

Long sentences are better for more controlled ideas and for developing points, as in the following examples.

When I think back to the summer of 1994, I don't think of the war that tore Yugoslavia apart, although it dominated the television news night after night; nor do I think of the World Cup and Ireland's heroic display; I cannot tell you whether we had a heat wave; or whether we dodged through summer showers, and tried to rub goosebumps from our T-shirted arms. No, none of these things come to mind. You see in the summer of 1994, I fell in love and out of love and I didn't have time for anything except her. My Maria.

or

Yet another report has been published to demonstrate that girls are outdoing boys when it comes to Leaving Cert results. Different groups are putting different spins on the statistics. The sociologists are highlighting that it proves that a laddish culture is marginalising boys when it comes to academic performance – there are few positive role-models for the studious teenager but plenty of geeky images come to mind in popular culture. The argument is that studying is seen as nerdy and so boys are encouraged to develop an image that stresses masculinity, rebellion and public performance. Consequently, boys tend to dominate class time in school, do less study at home, and pursue activities that involve competition and physical activity…

The best advice for the writing of sentences is to keep them simple and clear. You must be in control of the language you use, or it will control you.

VISUAL TEXT – Reading a visual text should take into account such factors as:

- Composition
- Colour
- Contrast
- Mood/atmosphere
- Theme
- Purpose
- Effect on audience

UNDERSTATEMENT – Another useful tool for every writer. It helps to vary expression and entertain the reader, and it can be useful in illustrating a point.

- *Man City spent a few quid in order to improve the squad.*
- *Remember there is little test at the end of sixth year.*
- *Hurling is somewhat skilful.*

FEATURES OF STYLE IN A TEXT

In every piece of writing that you encounter, always establish:

- The writer's purpose.
- The relationship with the reader.
- The style of writing.

Remember that **what** a writer says is linked to **how** he/she says it.

The following extracts should be read carefully.

Note how the various writers use language to:

- Reinforce the purpose.
- Communicate with the reader.
- Create mood/tone.
- Entertain the reader.

SAMPLE TEXTS AND EXERCISES

In responding to the texts, remember to:

- Read the questions carefully.
- Underline supporting references to make it easier to construct a response.
- Write an introductory paragraph that addresses the question and sets forth how you will answer.
- Write three or four paragraphs for each answer.
- Support each point with appropriate quotations.
- Conclude your answer appropriately.

TEXT 1

This extract from Charles Dickens's novel Hard Times *describes a fictional northern industrial city, Coketown.*

COKETOWN

by *Charles Dickens*

It was a town of red brick, or of brick that would have been red if the smoke and ashes had allowed it; but, as matters stood, it was a town of unnatural red and black like the painted face of a savage. It was a town of machinery and tall chimneys, out of which interminable circles of smoke trailed themselves for ever and ever, and never got uncoiled.

It had a black canal in it, and a river that ran purple with ill-smelling dye, and vast piles of building full of windows where there was a rattling and a trembling all day long, and where the piston of the steam-engine worked monotonously up and down, like the head of an elephant in a state of melancholy madness. It contained several large streets all very like one another, and many small streets still more like one another, inhabited by people equally like one another, who all went in at the same hours, with the same sound on the same pavements, to do the same work, and to whom everyday was the same as yesterday and tomorrow, and every year the counterpart of the last and the next.

EXERCISES

1. Features of style in the above extract.

Identify three features of style	Give an example	Comment on the effect
(i)		
(ii)		
(iii)		

2. Comment on how Dickens uses language to give us a negative impression of Coketown.

TEXT 2

This is the opening section of an article on coffee that appeared in the Irish Times.

WAKE UP AND SMELL THE COFFEE

Caffeine has been adored and dissected by artists, musicians and writers, such as Balzac (ratcheting up the doses to the extent of eating dry coffee powder), Rossini ("Coffee is an affair of fifteen or twenty days; just the right amount of time to write an opera"), Samuel Johnson (who drank 40 cups of tea a day), Voltaire, Beethoven and Goethe (who was indirectly responsible for isolating and naming it). It has served as the age-old prop of rebels without a cause, Greenwich Village bohemians, computer freaks and baggy-eyed new fathers. Once prohibited by royal edict and lamented as the bane of "coffee-house widows," held forth as a cure-all and source of health and creativity, and damned as a dangerous, even deadly drug, caffeine has always been a potent conversation starter. From early Stone-Age man getting his caffeine buzz by chewing up every conceivable part of caffeine-bearing plants, to modern researchers agitating over whether it can lead to birth defects and spontaneous abortion, the story of caffeine is a fountain of controversy from start to finish.

EXERCISES

1. Features of style in the above extract.

Identify three features of style	Give an example	Comment on the effect
(i)		
(ii)		
(iii)		

2. What stylistic features are used by the author to make this an interesting article on the subject of coffee?

TEXT 3

This is an extract from a speech by a leader of the Allied Forces during the Second Gulf War. On the eve of going into battle in March 2003 against Iraqi soldiers, Colonel Tim Collins of the Royal Irish Regiment (British army) delivered this speech to his troops.

WE GO TO LIBERATE

by Tim Collins

We go to liberate not to conquer. We will not fly our flags in their country. We are entering Iraq to free a people and the only flag which will be flown in that ancient land is their own. Show respect for them. There are some who are alive at this moment who will not be alive shortly. Those who do not wish to go on that journey, we will not send. As for the others, I expect you to rock their world. Wipe them out if that is what they choose. But if you are ferocious in battle, remember to be magnanimous in victory.

Iraq is steeped in history. It is the site of the Garden of Eden, of the Great Flood and the birthplace of Abraham. Tread lightly there. You will see things that no man could pay to see and you will have to go a long way to find a more decent, generous and upright people than the Iraqis. You will be embarrassed by their hospitality, even though they have nothing. Don't treat them as refugees for they are in their own country. Their children will be poor, in years to come they will know that the light of liberation in their lives was brought by you. If there are casualties of war then remember that when they woke up and got dressed in the morning, they did not plan to die this day. Allow them dignity in death. Bury them properly and mark their graves. The enemy should be in no doubt that we are his nemesis and that we are bringing about his rightful destruction. There are many regional commanders who have stains on their souls and they are stoking the fires of hell for Saddam. He and his forces will be destroyed for what they have done. As they die they will know their deeds have brought them to this place. Show them no pity.

EXERCISES

1. Features of style in the above extract.

Identify three features of style	Give an example	Comment on the effect
(i)		
(ii)		
(iii)		

2. What features make this a persuasive speech? Illustrate your answer with at least three examples of persuasive writing.

TEXT 4

The following text is an example of a well-written advertisement.

VISIT THE ICE HOTEL!

Imagine a hotel built from thousands of tons of snow and ice and re-built every winter – that is Icehotel, in the little village of Jukkasjarvi in Lapland, Sweden – 200km north of the Arctic Circle. The Icehotel continues a prosperous and prestigious climb as the world's largest hotel made completely of ice and snow.

This winter wonderland includes a reception, main hall, and ice-art exhibition and the world-famous "Absolut Ice Bar". Wonderful winter activities on offer are snow mobile safaris, dogsled tours, Sami cultural events, Northern Lights tour, cross-country skiing, traditional saunas, river dips, ice fishing, ice-water swimming and ice massage!

Stay overnight on a bed sculpted from a block of ice, keeping you nice and cosy with specially prepared reindeer skins. In the morning, you are woken with a welcoming hot drink followed by a hot sauna and then breakfast!

Icehotel is one of the truly unimaginable encounters the world has to offer today; if you travel somewhere truly spectacular and fascinating once in a lifetime – make it the Icehotel!

EXERCISES

1. Features of style in the above extract.

Identify three features of style	Give an example	Comment on the effect
(i)		
(ii)		
(iii)		

2. Comment on the main features in this text that might encourage a holiday-maker to stay at the Icehotel.

TEXT 5

In this extract from his autobiography, Pictures in my Head, *the Irish actor Gabriel Byrne recalls his first visit to the cinema in the 1950s. He was brought up by his grandmother.*

REEL MEMORIES

by *Gabriel Byrne*

From inside the doors I could hear loud voices, but not like the voices of real people, and I started to feel afraid and she looked at me and smiled and took my hand tightly again and said,

"There's nothing to be frightened of. It's only the pictures."

All around the foyer, there were painted photographs of men with thin black moustaches and women with bright red lipstick like my mother. Then the sentry pulled back the door and we were in darkness with the noise of those strange voices all around us. We edged our way along by a wall like blind people, me holding on to her coat for fear, till suddenly in an explosion of blinding colour, I saw before me the bluest sea I could imagine, and on it two huge boats with sails, sailing under a vast blueness of sky. I turned my head in terror into her body, and for an eternity of moments I dared not look again. When I opened my eyes I saw a light beam in the darkness and a voice asked for our tickets, as it came towards us. And with her arm around me, we followed the dancing light as it lit our way along the steps, 'til we found our seats and I sat down overwhelmed by the fear and the mystery and the magic of it all. But as the wonder grew, the terror died. And so I came to know the lovely dark womb of the picture-house for the first time.

Now the lights came slowly on from red stars of glass set high above us in the blue roof and around the walls from flickering lamps. And a snowy curtain that folded into silver trees as it slowly fell, covered the sea and the boat and the white writing and the voices.

"Was that a picture granny?"

"No, that was only an old trailer," she said.

EXERCISES

1. Features of style in the above extract.

Identify three features of style	Give an example	Comment on the effect
(i)		
(ii)		
(iii)		

2. Write a full appreciation of the style used in this extract from Gabriel Byrne's memoir. In your answer, refer to at least three features of style used by the writer.

This is a well-known piece of writing by the internationally regarded novelist Ernest Hemingway.

THE SUN ALSO RISES

by Ernest Hemingway

At noon on Sunday, the 6th July, the fiesta exploded. There is no other way to describe it. People had been coming in all day from the country, but they were assimilated in the town and you did not notice them.

I walked down the hill from the cathedral and up the street to the café on the square. It was a little before noon. The marble-topped tables and the white wicker chairs were gone. They were replaced by cast-iron tables and severe folding chairs. The café was like a battleship stripped for action.

Before the waiter brought the sherry, the rocket that announced the fiesta went up in the square. It burst and there was a grey ball of smoke high up above the Theatre Gayarre, across the other side of the plaza. The ball of smoke hung in the sky like a shrapnel burst, and as I watched another rocket came up to it, trickling smoke in the bright sunlight. I saw the bright flash as it burst and another cloud of smoke appeared. By the time the second rocket had burst, there were so many people in the arcade, that had been empty a minute before, that the waiter, holding the bottle high over his head, could hardly get through the crowd to our table. People were coming into the square from all sides, and down the street we heard the pipes and the fifes and the drums coming. They were playing the riau-riau music, the pipes shrill and the drums pounding, and behind them came the men and the boys dancing. When the fifers stopped they all crouched down in the street, and when the reed-pipes and the fifes shrilled, and the flat, dry, hollow drums tapped it out again, they all went up in the air dancing.

EXERCISES

1. Features of style in the above extract.

Identify three features of style	Give an example	Comment on the effect
(i)		
(ii)		
(iii)		

2. "Hemingway is a master of descriptive writing." Do you agree with this assessment? In your answer, refer to at least three features of style used by the writer.

VISUAL TEXT

INTRODUCTION

This chapter will focus on **Visual Texts**, which are the images as text. Comprehending A of the Leaving Certificate paper includes a question on a visual text. This can be asked about a text presented in one of the following formats:

1. Visual image or images by themselves.
2. Visual image with linked written text.

There are many different types of visual image from photographs to advertising posters to bar charts.

1. THE VISUAL TEXT

The **reading** of a visual text is a comprehension skill involving:

- Understanding
- Evaluating
- Interpretation

A study of a visual will reveal:

PURPOSE – Is there a clear purpose? Is it to convey information? To persuade? To affect our emotions?

THEME – Is there a message? Is it suggesting a viewpoint or attitude?

SUBJECT MATTER – A close study of the photo might reveal a narrative, or the composition might create a mood or atmosphere – pay attention to what is in the visual.

TONE/ATMOSPHERE – What feeling is created by the visual?

AUDIENCE – The effect on the viewer.

AUTHOR (PHOTOGRAPHER) – Does the photographer or illustrator or graphic artist reveal anything about themselves? Is the attitude neutral / biased / objective / fair?

Studying the composition of the image

A study of the composition of the image will necessitate an appreciation of the following aspects:

- Colour
- Composition
- Contrast
- Facial expression
- Close-up
- Background
- Foreground
- Focal point

TEXT 1

Study this photograph, which was taken by Robert Doiseau in 1950 in Paris. The original title is 'La baiser de L'Hotel de Ville' ('The kiss at the Hotel de Ville').

EXERCISES

1. In what way does the photographer make the couple the centre of attention?
2. Why has this photo continued to be popular?
3. Can you suggest reasons why black and white photographs are preferred by many photographers?

TEXT 2

Study this photograph which was taken by Anthony Suau in Cleveland, Ohio, in 2008. This was one of a series that the phographer did on the subject "The U.S. economy in crisis."

In this particular photograph, a police officer is making sure that a family has vacated a property after failing to pay the mortgage. In other words, the family has been evicted.

EXERCISES

1. What is the dominant mood created by this photograph?
2. Do you think the photographer had a purpose in taking this photograph? Give reasons for your answer.
3. Is it acceptable for photographers to be anything less than totally objective?

TEXT 3

Sometimes, you will be asked to compare images. Study the following images and answer the questions below.

1.

2.

3.

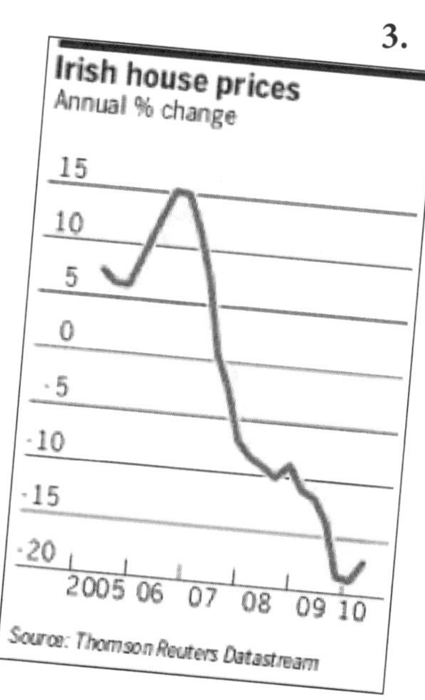

EXERCISES

1. Which of these images illustrates the 'property crisis' in Ireland in the strongest way? Give reasons for your answer.
2. Which image represents the crisis least successfully? Give reasons for your answer.
3. Imagine you are a journalist working on an article on the property crisis. Write a caption for each of the above images.

TEXT 4

Study these film posters and answer the questions that follow.

1.

2.

3.

EXERCISES

1. Taking all aspects of these posters into account, which do you think is the most successful poster in promoting a film? Take into account the genre of the film, the potential audience and other relevant factors. Give reasons for your answer.
2. What importance is attached to the text in each poster? Pay particular attention to the use of by-line.
3. Explain how you are attracted to particular movies. Is it by posters, reviews, trailers or word of mouth? Explain your answer in full.

TEXT 5

These photographs give somewhat different impressions of the lives of women. Study them and answer the questions that follow.

EXERCISES

1. Do you think this collection of photographs gives a positive view of women? You must support your answer by referring to the photographs.
2. Which of the photographs would you choose to illustrate an article on positive role models for young women? Give reasons for your answer.
3. Do any of the photographs in this collection depict women in a negative or stereotypical way? Explain your answer.

TEXT 1

This article written by Arminta Wallace appeared in the Irish Times *on the 10 November 2011. For the article, she interviewed the photographer Rich Gilligan. Read the written text, examine the visuals and answer the questions that follow.*

When you see the photograph of a writer on the jacket of their book, you don't tend to wonder how it came to be there. Jacket shots present themselves as a finished product – this is how I look, and that's the end of it.

But there's a story behind every photo. Who made the image? Was the writer happy in front of the camera or did the photographer struggle to get them to relax?

Ireland Literature Exchange yesterday launched postcards of eight contemporary Irish writers which it will distribute at book fairs all over the world from Frankfurt to Beijing.

The portraits were taken by the young Irish photographer Rich Gilligan; he tells how these literary luminaries looked from the other side of the lens.

JOHN BANVILLE

John has a little flat on the quays. I think he just goes there for work – it's very clean, organised, uncluttered. He was cool and really helpful. But I could tell he wanted me out as soon as I was in the door. It was like, have you got enough shots? Okay.

Don't get me wrong, he was great – and I knew what I wanted to shoot straight away because his desk space was so small and organised. It was perfect. For most people I'd try a couple of different options but with John I could see that it would work. Also, I could sense he was really busy and I didn't want to overstay my welcome. He was really intense, and I love when someone is that intense. As a photographer, there's nothing worse than when you go to shoot someone and it takes a long time to put them at ease. You can tell in a photograph – especially a formal portrait, where it's obvious that the sitter is aware of being photographed – if the person is not comfortable with the scenario. You can read body language so easily in photographs.

CLAIRE KILROY

She has this crow on her desk, which she talks to all the time. She says it features in two of her books. I wanted all the pictures to look contemporary, but since she's the youngest of the group I put more distance between myself and her than in the other shots, in order to capture the feel of that room. The whole scenario that she has – the glass cubes behind her, the desk, the crow – everything about it just works.

She has her laptop and notebooks there and that's where she spends most of her writing time. I didn't direct her at all, so the way she's sitting, and the movement – that totally came from her. But it took a long time to get it right. The light was really weird that day – whatever way the cloud cover was, it would get way too bright to shoot, so much so that we'd have to wait for clouds to come over and then try again.

But she was really patient. This is all stuff that makes sense in my head when I take a picture, but I'm sure to an outsider it could just seem completely OCD. But she had lots of ideas and gave a lot to it, and wanted to make the shot work.

COLM TÓIBÍN

When I went to Colm's house, I was immediately overwhelmed by the madness. It was great. So much clutter. Books upon books and notebooks and scrapbooks and bottles of wine and chocolates – crap everywhere. But aesthetically pleasing crap. He wanted to use a back room with nice bookcases, which was much tidier. We tried shooting there – but he has these huge bay windows at the front of the house and a desk where he seems to do most of his work and I was really drawn to that. He has a print by Richard Avedon and when I commented on it he ran off downstairs and reappeared with this original Avedon print of himself, shot in the 1980s, in New York I think. I nearly forgot about the job for a while and we chatted about Avedon. We only shot pictures for, I'd say, five minutes. I had a feeling what I'd got was really strong. He couldn't have been more open or helpful. He ended up giving me a whole collection of his books, all signed.

EXERCISES

1. Read the text that goes with each photograph. Which photograph do you think best reflects what you learn about the writer from the written text? Give reasons for your answer.
2. In studying the above photographs, what do the three writers have in common? Support your answer.
3. From reading and studying the images and text what do you learn about the photographer? Support your answer.

TEXT 2

This photograph was taken during the siege of Sarajevo during the Yugoslav war in the 1990s. The photographer was subsequently interviewed by the Guardian *newspaper on 2 October 2008. Study the photograph and read the text of the accompanying interview by Leo Benedictus.*

TOM STODDART'S BEST SHOT

I shot this picture in 1992, when the siege of Sarajevo was just beginning. It was one of the rare opportunities when the Serbian forces were allowing children to be bussed out by their parents to escape the shelling. This particular scene was re-enacted in the Woody Harrelson film *Welcome to Sarajevo.*

I saw the woman – who was very striking, with blue eyes – fighting back her tears. She had dressed her little boy in his finest kit, and it was obviously a very emotional time. There was also tension in the air; the Serbian forces were not averse to lobbing grenades into crowds. I shot a few frames up close and the picture was used around the world.

Two and half years ago, I got an email from a woman living in Perth in Australia saying: "I know who that woman is; she's my neighbour." So I went to Perth and tracked her down. Her name is Gordana Burazor, and Andre, the little boy, is now a teenager, and about 6ft 2in tall. Through all that time, I had always thought she just put the child on the bus, but in fact she managed to bribe her way on board as well.

She hates this picture. But when I'm talking to young photographers, I always say it is my kind of image: black and white, and you look into their eyes, trying to read what's going on in their minds, without them even noticing you.

She first saw the picture a few weeks after it was taken, and then periodically over the years, but never wanted to contact me. She said she hates it because she was trying to be completely dignified. And the one moment she did what she was trying to avoid – crying – was captured in this frame.

EXERCISES

1. What purpose is served by photographs such as this one taken in areas of conflict? Give reasons for your answer.
2. Do you think a black and white format adds to the power of this photograph? Read the text and study the photograph before writing your answer. Give reasons for your answer.
3. What is your reaction to both the photograph and the story the photographer tells us about it?

TEXT 3

The two visual images are of the film poster and the front cover of the novel of Children of Men *by English writer P.D. James. The written text is from the first page of the novel.*

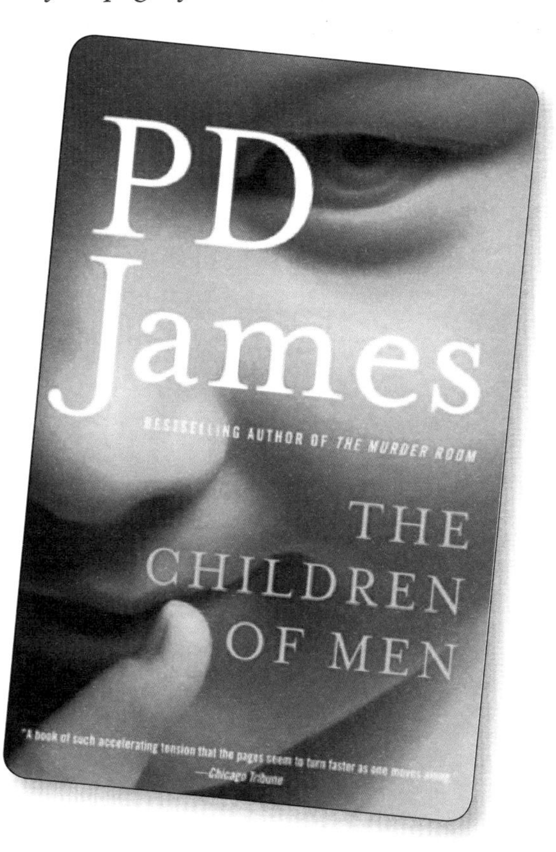

Friday, 1 January 2021

Early this morning, 1 January 2021, three minutes after midnight, the last human being to be born on earth was killed in a pub brawl in a suburb of Buenos Aires, aged twenty-five years, two months and twelve days. If the first reports are to be believed, Joseph Ricardo died as he had lived. The distinction, if one can call it that, of being the last the last human whose birth was officially recorded, unrelated as it was to any personal virtue or talent, had always been difficult for him to handle. And now he is dead. The news was given to us here in Britain on the nine o'clock programme of the State Radio Service and I heard it fortuitously. I had settled down to begin this diary of the last half of my life when I noticed the time and thought I might as well catch the headlines to the nine o'clock bulletin. Ricardo's death was the last item mentioned, and then only briefly, a couple of sentences delivered without emphasis in the newscaster's carefully non-committal voice. But it seemed to me, hearing it, that it was a small additional justification for beginning the diary today; the first day of a new year and my birthday.

EXERCISES

1. Examine the film poster and book cover for *Children of Men*. Having read the first page of the novel, which of the two visual images impresses you more? Give reasons for your answer.
2. Do you think the target audience would be the same or different for the book and film? Support your answer.
3. Read the opening page of the novel. How effective is it as an opening to a science fiction novel? Give reasons for your answer.

SECTION 3

COMPREHENDING B

5. Functional Writing

FUNCTIONAL WRITING

INTRODUCTION

You learned the importance of **functional writing** when studying for the Junior Certificate. Functional writing is constructing text with a clear sense of **purpose**. At Leaving Certificate level, you are expected to develop these skills.

For each task, there is **appropriate language**, which is affected by audience and content.

Always remember that attention to the task and correct expression are more important than the length of an answer.

Most of the sample texts in this chapter have been created by Fifth and Sixth Year students. They include examples of the following type of texts:

1. Letter to the editor of a newspaper.
2. Speech.
3. Report for a school website.
4. Diary for publication.
5. Emails.
6. Holiday advice.
7. Reviews (two).
8. Radio talk.

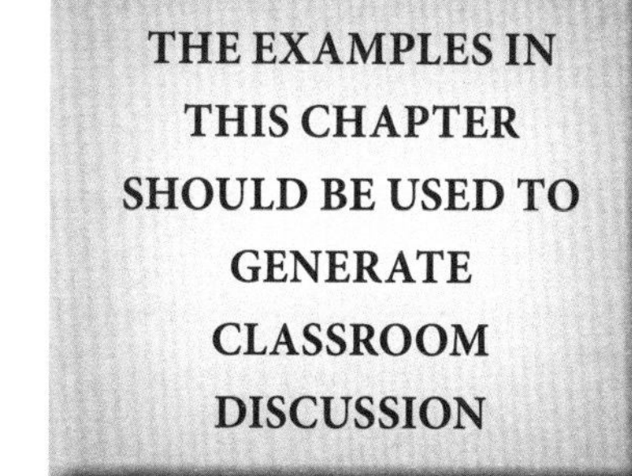

After reading them, you should consider whether the students have been successful in:

- Addressing the task.
- Using the appropriate language.
- Connecting with audience.
- Adopting the correct layout.

Each of the exercises that follow will give you plenty of practice, so that you will be able to cope with this section in the Leaving Certificate examination. Model your responses on the best examples. Remember that your reader will expect to be entertained by your creativity and ability with language.

In doing these assignments, think clearly about:

- The purpose.
- The audience.
- The shape and layout.
- Language, register and expression.

Among the most common functional tasks are:
REPORTS, SPEECHES, TALKS, DIARY ENTRIES, MEMOS, GUIDES, REVIEWS, OBITUARIES, LETTERS, ARTICLES.

As always, **planning and drafting are essential** when responding to an exercise on functional writing. Once you have completed a draft of your answer, you should ask yourself the following questions:

CHECKLIST ✓

- Have I completed the task?
- Is the language appropriate to the task?
- Are there any awkward expressions that I need to rephrase?
- Are there spelling, punctuation or grammar errors?
- Is the layout correct?
- Does it have a sense of its audience?
- Is there anything I could leave out?
- Is there anything else I should include?

Examples of Functional Writing

The examples that follow have been written by students in a range of styles from formal to informal.

1. LETTER TO EDITOR

The student's task is to write a letter for publication in a newspaper that counters negative views of teenagers. Before beginning, it is useful to examine and define the various components of this text.

PURPOSE: To challenge the newspaper on its negative depiction of teenagers.

AUDIENCE: General readership, but addressed to editor.

LAYOUT/STRUCTURE: Formal letter; clearly defined paragraphs.

LANGUAGE: Formal; persuasive writing including facts, rhetorical devices.

CONTENT: Reference to previous articles; effective use of facts.

Letter for publication in the *Roscommon Weekly Post*

7 Lake View Heights,
Ballinlough, ← address
Co. Roscommon.
7 November 2012

Madam, – I must take issue with the way your newspaper has been portraying young Irish people. In a series of articles, published on consecutive days, you give the impression that Irish teenagers are obese, addicted to Internet sites, socialise almost exclusively on Facebook, and (when not on the computer, presumably) binge drink. ← indicates reason for letter

Headlines such as "only 10% of Irish students read newspapers" are misleading. The implication is that we are ignorant of the world and do not have any interest in politics. You can accuse us of being cynical about our politicians, but isn't this a sign of our good judgement? The generation ahead of us has sold our birthright, hocked our futures, and sold out our sovereignty. ← strong sentence using triadic expression Maybe this explains our lack of interest. Our anger is softened by our indulgence in social networking. Who can blame us? ← rhetorical question

As for the accusation that we are "too lazy to meet and chat with each other and prefer to use Facebook", ← effective quotation offers strong response this is a misunderstanding of how we use social media. Facebook is not a way of avoiding friends. It is what we do in the evening before doing homework, for example. In fact, it gives us a chance to keep in touch, to stay abreast of news and gossip, and is a precursor for real social opportunities. You also had a misleading headline that we are so naïve as to meet up with people we met initially through Facebook. Not one of my friends has ever done this. It sounds more like something a lonely older person might do.

balanced point → I am in agreement that there has been a worrying escalation in the numbers of young people who are obese. Rather than use this fact as a rallying call for action to be taken, you merely use it to criticise young people. Teenage obesity is a medical and social

thoughtful

persuasive argument

problem. All western countries are having to face it. Some Nordic countries favour putting a "fat tax" on some foods. Their governments are taking action. Who feeds us? Who produces the food? Who sells the food? Surely it is not the fault of teenagers. It is a wider problem that politicians and parents have not addressed. Teenagers are consumers, not producers, so maybe the food that is available to us is part of the problem. Schools, by and large, do not supply us with healthy food, so it is hypocritical to blame us.

Yes, we do live sedentary lives. Maybe the lack of facilities goes some way to explaining this. That said, I don't know the statistics but I would be surprised to learn that today's children, on average, take less exercise than those of previous times. The local rugby, GAA and soccer clubs are flourishing.

supports point

structure signals the end

Finally, you gave a lot of space to the "Crisis of Binge Drinking Teens" (as your headline put it). Ireland has a problem with drink. This has little to do with age. Social occasions are built around the consumption of alcohol. Funerals, weddings, birthdays, sporting losses and wins all involve gallons of drink. Attempts to tackle this must be a little more imaginative than blaming teenagers. Who are our role models? I suggest that we are following a trend set by our fellow (adult) Irish men and women. Hopefully, we will be the generation to change our nation's attitude to drink. It is a tall order (forgive the pun)!

use of humour

strong conclusion

Your series of articles no doubt gained you extra readers, but at the cost of the truth. We are the children of a generation that ruined this country. I think we are its greatest hope. Don't knock us. Trust us instead.

sign off

Yours

H. Byrne

EXERCISES

1. What makes this an effective letter to the newspaper?
2. Write a letter to a national newspaper on a current topic that you feel strongly about.

2. SPEECH

The student's task is to write a speech to be delivered to his or her classmates on why reality television shows appeal, or do not appeal, to audiences. Before beginning, it is useful to examine and define the various components of this text.

PURPOSE: To explain the appeal of reality television/keep audience focused and entertained.

LAYOUT/STRUCTURE: Speech is tightly structured in paragraphs with a strong opening and conclusion.

AUDIENCE: Classmates and teacher.

LANGUAGE: Conversational; informal but aware of class rules.

CONTENT: References to a range of popular programmes.

introduction strikes balance between informal and formal

Good afternoon girls, and Mr Madden! I want to share my guilty pleasure with you. Reality TV shows are the most exciting programmes on the box at the moment. We all say they are rubbish, we make fun of them all the time, but they are addictive and appeal to us on so many levels. Aren't they the kind of distraction we need in this year of serious exams, form-filling and pressure? If we are honest, I bet each of us in this room has one that we never miss. Even, you sir, no doubt you never miss *Masterchef*, do you?

colloquial phrase

focus on task

rhetorical question and triadic expression

What other shows are so entertaining, so cruel, so controversial and so utterly unmissable? The BBC version of *The Apprentice* (forget TV3's poor imitation – "Mr Cullen, you're fired") is a class programme. Forget product placement, and the annoying so-called experts, it is so entertaining to watch the small-minded and selfish behaviour of contestants 'dissing' their 'colleagues' in order to appear as budding business people. No other programme gives such insight into how nasty people can be in order to succeed. That moment when Sir Alan raises his finger to issue his dismissal is akin to a Roman Emperor of old giving the thumbs down to a doomed gladiator. Be honest, don't we all relish the power that he has?

humour

alliterative phrasing

If all the business blather is not to your liking, then how can you not like Gok Wan and his attempts to turn ugly ducklings, and ageing ducks for that matter, into glorious swans? Doesn't *How to Look Good Naked* appeal to our desire to be attractive, to find out the secrets of looking beautiful without the hassle of going to Weightwatchers or the expense of surgery? It is one programme I can watch with mum and share real banter.

colloquial phrasing for benefit of audience

knowledge of topic

But when it comes to the king of reality TV shows, it is hard to ignore the *X-Factor*. The show has everything: the rags-to-riches stories; the judges' eccentric personalities; the villains and heroes, tears and tantrums. Yes, I know the cynical girls out there will say that the show manipulates its audience. Yes, of course, it does. From Monday to Saturday, the tabloids are drip fed gossip about the contestants. We learn about their tantrums, misbehaviour, their backgrounds, being brought up by a granny on Merseyside, petty squabbling. This is done in an attempt to boost ratings, and it succeeds. As the show builds to its Christmas climax, ratings soar. But you must admit, it works. Who in Ireland was not rooting for Mary Byrne when she appeared? Who actually liked the eccentric Wagner (even Louis, his mentor couldn't pronounce his name correctly)? Are any of us now cringing that we actually thought Jedward were cute?

This show has everything: the element of competition, suspense, arguments and controversy. On the judging panel, Cheryl and Kelly are like sisters we would love to have; Simon resembles a cranky but likeable uncle; Gary Barlow is like one of our big sisters' hot boyfriend; and Louis, well Louis Walsh is like a crazy granny who gets way too emotional. The formula of this show is perfect. It's not popular for its music. If I want that I have my iPod. The appeal, the secret of its attraction with audiences, is the way it becomes a talking point. Sometimes I watch it with friends - girls, you know the fun of a girls' night in on Saturday watching the live show. If I watch it on my own I spend half the time ferociously texting friends with my comments.

humour

Because reality TV shows are unscripted, and for the most part live, anything can happen. There is also the added attraction of the interaction between the programme and its audience; the live audience and the viewing public are as much as part of the show as the judges and contestants.

And if these three programmes are not to your liking, then there is always *Jersey Shore, Only Way Is Essex* or *I'm a Celebrity Get Me out of Here*. OK, I admit these are pretty dumb, but they appeal to our nosiness, our nastiness and our cruelty. Be honest, girls, admit it, reality TV is the only show in town.

connects with audience

Desperate Housewives and *Madmen* are great, but keeping up with the storylines is sometimes too much like work. If we want complicated plot development, we have *Hamlet* to keep us going, don't we, Mr. M? For the pure joy of escapism, we have reality TV.

reminder of context

Thanks for listening.

EXERCISES

1. Comment on how expression and content would make this an effective talk when delivered in front of a class.
2. Write a speech to be delivered to your class on the topic of what people's clothes say about them.

3. REPORT

A school is constructing a library. The principal has asked students to make submissions on the school's website, outlining their suggestions as to how they would like to see a school library. Before beginning, it is useful to examine and define the various components of this text.

PURPOSE: To make suggestions in a persuasive manner.

AUDIENCE: Principal and possibly senior teachers.

LAYOUT/STRUCTURE: Email/ paragraphs/ clearly identified points.

LANGUAGE: Formal/clear sentences.

TO: Principal, headman@schoolmail.ie
SUBJECT: Library
From: Sile Graham, student, sileg@pmail.ie

formal introduction note layout

As a Sixth-Year student in this school, I have very definite ideas as to what a school library should be like. I feel that the following recommendations should be given serious consideration. They are based on my experience, having spent five years at Bookside Commmunity School.

clearly expressed points in logical order

First, the library should be set aside as a special space in the school for students to be able to study in a quiet and relaxed atmosphere. I would recommend that the library should be available to students an hour before and an hour after school for this purpose. This facility will enable senior students to use their time effectively. At the moment, there is nowhere that students can do work before 8:30am when the classrooms are opened.

language is precise

Secondly, the library could serve a social function and become an attractive place for students to meet in a semi-formal environment. At lunch time, this would be the perfect place for the students who do not go out or play sport to meet. I can picture a place with comfortable seating, a warm atmosphere, and plenty of interesting reading material. Daily newspapers and interesting magazines should be provided for students to keep up with the political, business and entertainment news of the day. This would help with subjects such as English and Business. A shelf should also contain up-to-date novels for those who like to read as a hobby. There are plenty of students who like books such as the *Twilight* series. I would recommend plenty of books suitable for the younger students as well, especially for the Transition-Year students, who have so much free time.

practical advice

Thirdly, I think that an area of the library could be provided with a number of computers for the use of the students. This would aid research and could be useful for students. History students could work on their special topic. There should be access to the Internet. Transition-Year students would benefit enormously as they always have projects to work on. Of course, several websites would have to be blocked, but technology is available to do this.

Fourthly, during the day the library space might be used as an alternative to classrooms.

In the evenings, the area could be used for debates and lectures. I also propose the establishment of a book club. This could meet on the last Friday of every month. It would be a good opportunity for teachers to mix with us and share their passion for reading in an informal environment.

I would suggest that senior students could monitor the library to ensure it is kept clean and tidy. If the school makes us (the students) responsible for the library, then it will be respected. The running of the library might be given to Transition-Year students.

Thank you for taking the time to consider these proposals. I sincerely hope that future pupils will benefit from having a modern school library here at Bookside.

shows understanding of the purpose of a school library

original and practical suggestions

effective conclusion

EXERCISES

1. What evidence is there that this submission has been given a lot of thought before been sent to the principal?
2. Your principal has asked the students in your school to submit suggestions for a suitable person who should be invited to open the new senior wing of your school that has just been completed. Give your suggestion and write out the reasons for proposing this person.

   or

   The Department of Education website has announced a national competition asking all students in Ireland for suggestions as to how this country can best commemorate the 1916 rising. Send in your suggestion, giving reasons why you think your proposal should be adopted.

4. DIARY FOR PUBLICATION

What follows is a student's diary detailing a school trip abroad to be published in the school magazine. This will be different to a personal diary – it is not a private record and has a specific audience. Before beginning, it is useful to examine and define the various components of this text.

PURPOSE: To inform, amuse, entertain.

AUDIENCE: Parents, teachers, and fellow pupils.

LANGUAGE: Informal, and conversational, present tense, immediate past, lively expression.

STRUCTURE and LAYOUT: Dates placed at the beginning of each entry. Entries made at the end of each day. Chronological order. Avoids a short story approach. The use of puns and frequent references to teachers help to structure the entries.

CONTENT: The main events of the tour with personal observations and reflections, short descriptions.

clearly identified diary entries →

Feb. 12:

We assembled at the school at 5am this morning and never was less noise heard from 29 pupils and three teachers. Journey to airport was uneventful, as far as the sleeping pupils were concerned. Mr White read his Irish Times and Miss English her novel. The flight was delayed, but this proved to be a blessing in disguise, as we met up with St Marks – they're going skiing. We're going "on an educational visit to the fountain of civilization", to quote Ms Talin.

← personal tone helped by conversational language – relaxed and informal

← humorous names makes the diary interesting and witty

Aer Lingus Flight EI567 took off from a miserable Dublin and landed in a sunny, but not too warm, Rome.

On the way to the hotel, we had our first taste of real Italian pizzas. Perfecto.

present tense used correctly here to make the entries realistic →

My feet are sore because, after a quick visit to hotel, we made our way to ancient Rome. Mr White gave a pep talk told us not to go "roaming off" – he's so funny.

Becky, Vicky and Grainne paid a man dressed as a gladiator to pose for a photo with them. It cost €5. Ecstatic screams of delight rocked Rome when he put his arms around them.

Dasher wanted to know why Rome looked different in Gladiator – but even he was impressed when we got to the Colosseum. Ms Talin "ooed" and "goshed" the whole time. Burke and Tansey had "roamed off".

← humour the use of puns is used as a structuring device

Dinner was great. It's now 10:30pm. I am so beat. Sum morto, as they probably don't say.

Feb. 13, 4:00pm:

Today has been amazing. The coach took us to Pompeii. In class, we had heard about it, we had even seen a video, but the real thing is amazing. It even blew Dasher away. Now, he wants to study Latin. Poor Ms Talin!

Caroline wanted to know if the volcano was safe; we all laughed until the guide told us that it erupts in patterns of 500 years and the last was about... 500 years ago. The preserved corpses were deadly; thanks Mr White, you are a bad influence!

humorous anecdote

In the late afternoon, we were taken to a leisure complex. One of the teachers was heard to say to the driver, "It should tire them out." No way. Swam in an Olympic pool. We were impressed by Ms English. She dived from the top of the highest platform and we learned that she competed in the Olympics in 1976. The things you learn on school trips. Ms Talin was right; it is educational.

12 midnight:

Becky, Vicky and James had planned an impromptu party, but the teachers beat us to it. They organised a disco for us, together with an Italian school. It was great. It seems Ms English lived in Italy in the 1970s. What will we learn next? Great night. Parlo molto Italiano with the signorinas.

Feb. 14:

coherent structure

Last day. Beautiful drive along the coast. Ms English was not with us. Mr White said she has personal business. Will we ever find out? Rumours spread around the bus about her life before teaching. Becky went to sit with Whitey, but couldn't learn a thing. What is it with teachers and their secrets? Colin said that it was like being back home except for the good weather, the amazing food, the volcano, incredible buildings. So not much like home really.

the puns help to structure the piece

Great groans went up when we saw the airport signs. Each one was like the tick of an alarm clock reminding us the holiday was coming to an end. The flight back was very plain. (This punning has to stop). Ms English still missing.

slightly more formal as the article is for school magazine

P.S. The above is a real and accurate account of our school trip and any relation to persons living or dead is purely deliberate. Thanks to the teachers for giving up their mid-term break to give us such a great time. A special thanks to Ms Talin for her educational insights, to Mr White for his military planning and organization, and to Ms English for all her surprises. Grazie.

By the way, Ms English did return home shortly after us. It seems she was interviewed by an Italian television station, which was doing a programme about famous athletes who lived in Italy in the 1970s.

EXERCISES

1. Do you think a school magazine/yearbook is an appropriate publication for this diary? Give reasons for your answer.
2. Write three or four day diary entries on *one* of the following topics:

   A teenager whose family is snowbound in the worst weather this century.

   or

   First few days of a new school year.

   or

   First few days in a new job.

5. E-MAILS

This is an email sent home to parents by an exchange student. Unlike the email report earlier, this is an informal text. Before beginning, it is useful to examine and define the various components of this text.

PURPOSE: To communicate with parents; give information about the exchange; record impressions; entertain.

AUDIENCE: The parents of the writer.

LANGUAGE: Informal.

STRUCTURE/LAYOUT: The dates give it a natural chronological order. There is also a narrative element as we see relationships develop.

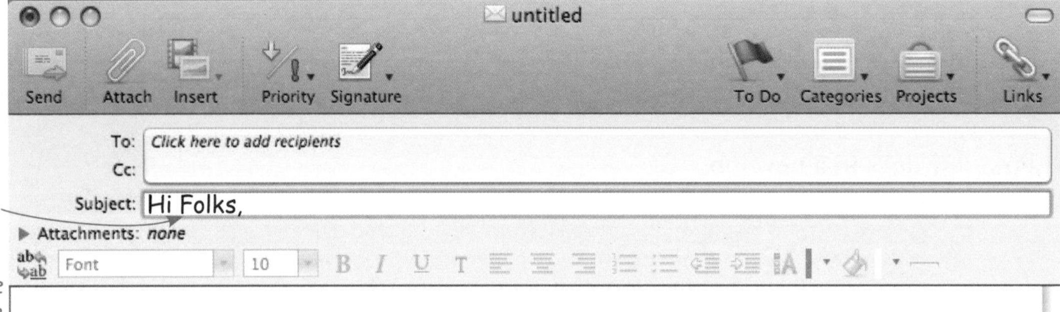

informal greeting suitable to e-mail language appropriate to audience

Really glad that you gave me this laptop because keeping in touch is not going to be easy. The mobile eats up credit. I am going to be very disciplined (doesn't sound like me, but give me the benefit, eh) and will keep a daily record of my week in France. Believe me, it is a relief to think and write in English.

purpose clearly stated

You probably want to know about the French family and the living conditions, the weather, food, etc. Monsieur Houlot collected me at Lyons airport. Very polite, very French, very hard to understand. I think he expected a student of French from Ireland to be able to converse as freely as himself in French. He was disappointed. The journey to his house was a bit nervy; I could just about get the gist of what he said and could only reply with **Oui** and **non**.

correct use of tenses diary reflects on events of the day

effective use of triadic expression

The Houlots live in an **appartement** on the **sixieme etage**. It is huge. Madam Houlot, Patricia, is very nice and has a little English; well, actually quite a lot. They have one daughter, Marie, who is my age. I don't know if we will get on. For the next week, we have to spend all day together.

French words give the diary a sense of reality

introduces characters in a natural and effective way

I was very surprised at dinner because between saying "**bon appetit**" and actually eating, they stopped to say a prayer. I am not sure if this was for my benefit. When they asked me to say the '**priere**', I hadn't a clue what they meant. I thought they were talking about the starter. Then Monsieur Hulot joined his hands and I understood. I was so embarrassed I couldn't think of anything to say in any language. So, I just put my hands together and closed my eyes and whispered silently. I think I got away with it.

effective andecdote

Food was superb. They all had wine. Except me. In the evening, the quiet Marie took me to meet her friends. During the day, she seemed boring, but when we went out, she transformed. I dressed in my usual casual clothes, but she arrived in the hall fully armed for a night out. **Tres embarrassment**. Her friends were very nice, very polite. But I was a fish out of water. Hope they don't think we Irish are usually so unstylish.

It's now late, so I won't go on. Miss you. Make sure you look after Gingy.

Love, Sue

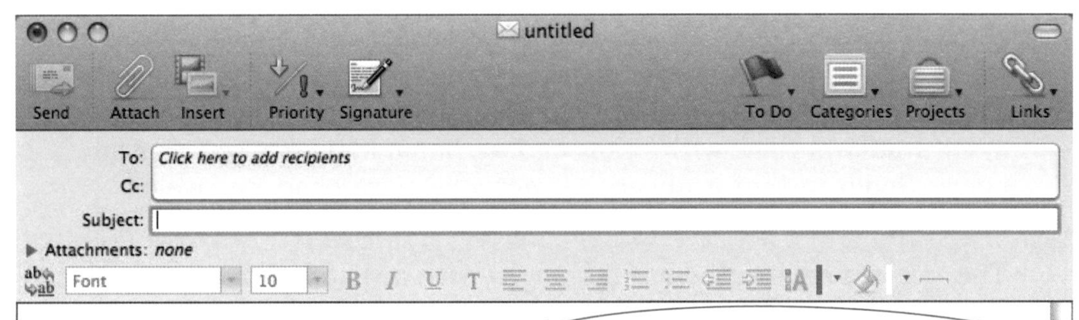

First day at school: what a nightmare! So different to Irish school. The classes are chaotic. Constant chatter. The teachers seem relaxed and dress very casually. Marie really is a pain, though. She is supposed to look after me, but spends her time with her own friends.

Acceptable use of informal expression

email gives insight into feelings and attitudes

We had most of the afternoon off, so we went into the centre of the town. Luckily, we bumped into a group of Irish boys. I kind of got my own back on Marie by speaking with them and ignoring her. Dinner was fine. No prayer this time. I noticed that Marie did absolutely no homework and lounged in front of the most boring television programmes. I went to my room and tried to do the maths exercises.

insight into the writer's character

Marie went out after dinner and I stayed in. I think Marie and her mum had a fight. Patricia told me about a summer she spent in London when she was young. She is looking after me well.

It's only ten, but I am **tres fatigue**.

Love, Sue

Interesting observations and personal response to the school

In school today, I had to speak to the class about life in Ireland. This was during the English language period. It was weird being in a class listening to 20 students speaking English with French accents. Some were actually good. I must say it was the best time I have spent so far. After class, a group sat with me for lunch and I did feel better.

In the afternoon, I volunteered to do the maths homework on the board and Marie suddenly changed her tune. For the rest of the day, she has been all over me. Now, she knows I am useful.

I helped her with the homework after dinner and she has been much nicer.

Thinking of you all. Make sure Gingy gets to sleep on my bed.

Love, Sue

Today was great. Marie's class had a tour to a local cinema where they were showing a film – it was **Shakespeare in Love**, in English, with French subtitles. The weird thing is I followed the subtitles. Without knowing it, I am actually speaking a lot of French.

Tonight at dinner, I told Patricia all about our day, while Marie hardly spoke to her parents. But she did open up to me later and told me that Patricia is not her real mother. Her father remarried after his wife – her real mother – died when she was eight. Beginning to understand her and actually do like her now. She is more vulnerable than she appeared at first.

Character development

Love, Sue

Au Revoir, La France. Last school day and last night at the Houlots', and I'm ready to return. I was surprised that in the English class many students came with cakes and we had a little party. I was so happy. Realised that my French is actually quite good, and we all switched from English to French and back.

structure

The Houlots celebrated our last night with a visit to the restaurant. They really have been kind. I was glad you gave me Irish homemade sweets to give to them as a goodbye present; they really loved them.

Marie surprised me again by saying she was sad that I was leaving. I was even more surprised that she had a present for me – a nice little painting of Lyons. I promised her that she would be welcome in Dublin – hope you don't mind.

Looking forward to seeing you all at the airport tomorrow! Can't wait!

strong ending

Love, Sue

EXERCISES

1. Do you agree that the emails above give us a good understanding of the student's exchange trip to France? Give reasons for your answer.
2. Write a series of e-mails home by a teenager who is spending a short trip abroad.

   or

   Write an on-line diary describing a difficult week in the life of a Leaving Cert student.

6. HOLIDAY ADVICE

Before beginning, it is useful to examine and define the various components of this text.

PURPOSE: To inform, advise.

AUDIENCE: General public, but might be more specific, depending on type of tourist and resort.

LANGUAGE: Clear, factual, objective.

STRUCTURE and **LAYOUT**: Use **block lettering** for important places; **headings** for paces of interest, eating out, travel, etc.

CONTENT: Useful information about travel, places to eat, places to visit. Tips and advice.

GUIDE TO SINTRA

If you are staying on the coast near Lisbon and feel you need a break from beach-life, you should treat yourself to a day in the nearby beautiful town of Sintra. This is one of the jewels of Portugal and is all the more fantastic for being hidden away from the seaside resorts. It is surprisingly easy to access. Trains run on the hour from Lisbon's main station (tickets cost €1.50). If you prefer a more picturesque journey, you can travel on the local bus, which meanders its way through sleepy towns. Bus travel is incredibly cheap; tickets can be bought on board for 50 cent.

language is clear and precise

connects with the reader

practical advice

What surprises all visitors to the wonderful village of Sintra is its opulence. It was once the summer residence of the Kings of Portugal. In the summer months, the air is refreshingly cool and the area has fantastic woodland paths that provide the traveller with scenes of great natural beauty. In the nineteenth century, Sintra attracted many famous people, including Lord Byron who celebrated it in a poem.

effective adjectives

historical facts

It is recommended that you take a walk around the ancient Moorish walls. The Moors ruled this area for hundreds of years and these walls are a reminder to us of Europe's diverse history. Your imagination will be overwhelmed and soon you will imagine yourself transported back centuries.

A visit to the King of Portugal's residence is optional. If ancient weaponry is your thing, you might like to pay the admission price (€10). Alternatively, a visit to the Museu de Arte Moderna is a must for those who are interested in contemporary art.

language is less formal

After your exertions, you will be feeling somewhat peckish. The town has a number of places to eat. The menus are in English and Portuguese. In the afternoon, after you have had a look at the many craft shops, you should take a stroll through the woods. The pathways are well signposted and you will be impressed by the area's natural beauty.

more practical advice

The best way to travel back towards Lisbon is by the mini-railway which charts a journey through unspoilt woodland, arriving at a spectacular surfing beach. If you enjoy swimming, we suggest you bring a towel and swim wear. A regular bus service connects this area with Lisbon.

Our Top Tip: Avoid travelling to Sintra on a Sunday. It is popular spot with locals and the roads can get very congested. We do not recommend this excursion to parents with very young children.

useful advice

EXERCISES

1. What aspects of the above article would a traveller to the area find useful? Support your answer with reference to the article.
2. The local tourist office has asked you to compile a short guide to your area. Submit your response.

7 (a). REVIEW

The following is a review of computer game. Before beginning, it is useful to examine and define the various components of this text.

PURPOSE: To inform and review; give advice and recommendation.

AUDIENCE: Specific audience (gamers) but the expression makes it appeal to a general reader.

STRUCTURE/LAYOUT: Begins with a personal anecdote, but the review goes into detail.

LANGUAGE: Mixture of impersonal and personal language, suitable to a young audience.

21/12/12. Ominous-sounding? Doom-laden visions of the apocalypse? Just another date in the calendar? The Mayans didn't think so and their calendar ends at that point.

introduction grabs the reader's attention

Last year, when I was still in the time warp that is transition year, the doomsday prophets were again at work. A press release had just announced that on the 11/11/11 all life would suddenly change. Study and social life would come to a stop. Well, for a percentage of the population anyhow. What I hear you ask was in that press release? The second Friday in November was the date chosen for the long-awaited-longest running most engrossing role-play game of our time. You got it: Skyrim. That date became a beacon of light at the end of a transition year tunnel of boredom. The pressure of fifth year was soothed by the knowledge that a new era of gaming would begin. 300 hours of hi-definition adventures in the mountainous tundra of Skyrim was the promised land.

personal anecdote that might appeal to fellow gamers lets us know something about the reviewer

purpose becomes clear

And so it came to pass. Last Friday, I got my hands on a copy of the fifth game in the epic "Elder Scrolls" series. Suddenly, the yammering voice of my elders telling me to accomplish something with my life, start taking studies seriously, were silenced. The only sound I would hear would be the whish of enchanted weaponry (in Dolby) slicing through the many mystical creatures set to stand in my path.

archaic language is appropriate to the topic

effective vocabulary

On the fateful Friday, I bid farewell to normal life. My non-gaming friends, and girlfriend, were blotted out. I was ready to do battle. Having ripped the annoying cellophane from the box (it seemed to take hours), stripped down to T-shirt and boxers (battle attire for all serious gamers), I was now waiting expectantly for the DVD to load. Suddenly, a dragon swooped across the screen and I was immersed in a brave new world.

I was not disappointed. This game really is the pinnacle, the apotheosis, the Everest of all games. The makers of this game (mythological craftsmen themselves) have done justice

opinion stated

to the series. The narrative, special effects, sound quality, are all exceptional. Your character is no longer limited to basic levelling up, but can now improve and gain perks on each level in anything from blacksmithing and archery to magical restoration and destruction. In other words, the more you play, the more sophisticated and more advanced the gaming becomes. Non-gamers will not understand the enthusiasm, obsessive behavior, pure dedication of us aficionados.

facts

good awareness of readers

If you have played any of the games in the series, you will not be disappointed. The €54.99 is money well spent. It can be played on X-Box , PC or PS3Y. Nay-sayers, who believe this game is addictive and consumes ambition, certainly make a fair point. But would I have ever become the most powerful wood elf in all of Tamriel, were it not for this game?

important facts

Andrew Cullen, Fifth-Year student

EXERCISES

1. Assess the above review in terms of its effectiveness and usefulness. Take into account the style and content of the review.
2. Write a review of a visit to a restaurant or a concert. This review is to appear in a magazine for teenagers.

7 (b) REVIEW

The following is a review of the well-known prison-drama movie, *The Shawshank Redemption*. Before beginning, it is useful to examine and define the various components of this text.

PURPOSE: To inform, to give opinion, recommend or criticise.

AUDIENCE: Teenagers/young adults.

LAYOUT/STRUCTURE: Paragraphs; information box.

LANGUAGE: Somewhat formal but appropriate to audience.

CONTENT: Factual content about the plot and actors, but also opinion and recommendation or otherwise.

THE SHAWSHANK REDEMPTION (1994)

142 MINUTES

Starring *Tim Robbins* (Andy Dufresne),
Morgan Freeman ('Red' Redding)
Bob Gunton (Warden Norton).

Directed and written by
Frank Darabont; based on the short story *'Rita Hayworth and Shawshank Redemption'* by Stephen King.

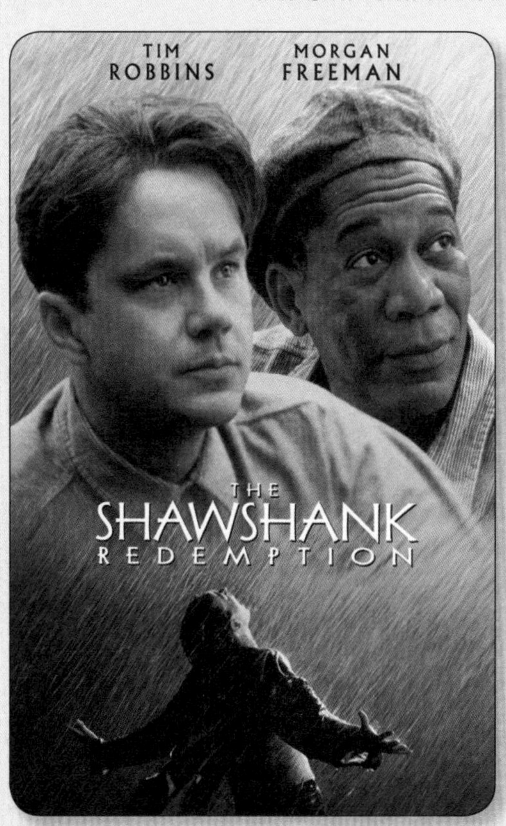

I wonder if films set in prisons have a special appeal to young people because schools are a similar, controlled environment, run by authority figures, where inmates are brutalised and suffer injustice. Maybe not. Whatever. The *Shawshank Redemption* is my favourite film for many reasons.

establishes a personal tone

effective introduction

When I was in transition year, this incredibly engrossing film transformed a very dull day. I was so deeply moved that I bought the DVD (a real bargain at €6.99, I might add). It is one of the very few films I can watch over and over again.

What is the appeal of this heart-warming film? Firstly, it is the story of one man's triumph over adversity. The prison is a cruel, unfair and violent place. The main character, banker Andy

clear statement of theme

Dufresne (played by Tim Robbins), has been found guilty of the murder of his wife and her lover and sentenced to life imprisonment. He seems unsuited to prison life. He befriends Red Redding, played by Morgan Freeman. Freeman won an Oscar and his performance is stunning. It is his voiceover that captivates us first. In a gentle and friendly manner, he explains prison life and tells us how he first met Andy.

important facts about actors

The relationship between Red and Andy is at the heart of the movie. Red is an experienced prisoner who seems to understand prison life. The other inmates all seem to like him, as we do. He has a network of connections, which he uses to get inmates what they need in exchange for cigarettes and money. The quiet Andy asks Red to get him a poster of the film actress Rita Hayworth and a rock hammer, which he seems to use to pursue his hobby which is geology. Of course, we soon learn that he has another use for these (I am not going to spoil it for you).

good advice for all reviewers

The villain of the film is the Chief Warden of the prison, who is a Bible-reading hypocrite. He is cruel and corrupt. He exploits the prisoners, getting them to work for local businesses while he pockets their pay. In a great scene, he is outwitted by Andy.

Each character has to make the best of what they have to survive in prison. Red's likeable character means he is at ease with people and has no enemies. Andy uses his knowledge of finance to do the tax returns of the warders, including the Chief. This is almost too successful as he becomes indispensible to the authorities, which means he will never be moved.

There are some very sad moments, such as when we see a man who has spent his entire life in prison being unable to adjust to life outside. We also see the cruelty of the warder as he allows the prisoners to be abused.

Without giving away the ending, I will say that the action keeps you on the edge of your seat until the very end.

If you want to experience a film that is dramatic, incredibly moving, has fantastic dialogue and superb acting, I recommend you watch this film. Strangely, it was not an immediate success with cinema-goers, but has now established itself as one of the best movies of all time. Treat yourself to this modern classic.

strongly worded recommendation

EXERCISES

1. A successful review should contain a mixture of fact and opinion; having read it, the reader should a clear understanding of the subject under review. Do you think the above review is a successful one?
2. Write a review of one of the following: your favourite film, CD, computer game or book. This review is to appear in a magazine published in your school. Your readership will consist of fellow pupils, but parents and teachers will be encouraged to buy it.

8. RADIO TALK

The following text is a talk on the importance of being positive; it is to broadcast on a local radio station. Before beginning, it is useful to examine and define the various components of this text.

PURPOSE: To inform/explain/persuade.

AUDIENCE: General audience composed of adults setting off to work/people at breakfast/one's peers.

STRUCTURE/LAYOUT: Speech should hook readers with a snappy thought-provoking introduction; clearly laid-out ideas in paragraphs/strong conclusion.

LANGUAGE: Conversational but not overly informal.

establishes rapport with listeners!

acceptable slang terms

context

Good morning, listeners. 99FM has asked me – a senior student at Ballinoige College – to prepare a few words on being positive for the 'Today's Thought' slot. On a damp and dreary February morning, in the middle of a recession you probably think that being positive is not easy. However, new days do begin with a little light, spring follows after every winter. There is always hope, even in the darkest hour.

conversational tone

interesting anecdote

On Sunday, I visited my grandmother, a fit and bright-eyed eighty-one year old. She told me that when she was sixteen she was put on a train to Dublin and spent the next ten years working in a shop. She married, returned home to Ballinoige, and reared eight children. She lived through war rationing, saw most of her children emigrate and there was no health care. Times were tough for all, but especially for a woman.

appeals to listeners

Listeners, people like my gran did not allow poverty and lack of opportunity defeat them. She got through it. And what does she attribute this to? She had a belief that things would get better and a strong faith in God.

relevance

use of personal pronouns create connection with audience

creates link between the generations

As we face this bleak February day, we should be glad that spring is here, the days are lengthening and soon the lambs will be seen bouncing across our fields. Even if we are awakening in darkness, we can put on a light. When gran set up home first, there was no electricity in the village. As you wait for the toast to pop up, or for the kettle to boil, I am sure you are not shivering in a house with no central heating. The brightness of our lives shows that we should be positive. Ireland is relatively prosperous.

I am sure the eight o'clock news will tell us of more lay-offs, more bad news from the European Central Bank, trouble at home and abroad. What will not be reported are the good, life-affirming stories that happen every single day. Here is my news for today:

Yesterday, in our local hospital a baby was born. This amazing miracle was overseen by a team of professional medics in a wonderful hospital. I am an aunt and my sister is very happy to be a mother.

Yesterday, there were no major accidents on our roads, goods were delivered, children brought to school and returned to loving parents. Homework was done, dinners eaten and bedtime stories told.

In sport, the local GAA team played a match at which there was no fighting. Thirty fit players gave their all in a wonderful sporting spirit. And we won. ← original idea

These stories will not make the national news, but every day people celebrate successes, large and small. Great things happen that go unreported. There is more good than bad in the world. People greet each other warmly in shops, old people are still helped across the road and love is still being shared. Listeners, do not become battered by negative thoughts. Of course there are terrible things, but I also know that every problem has a solution. If we look around us, we can also find a reason to be happy. As a Leaving Certificate student, I know that if I work and do my best, things will be OK.

theme

When I was ten, I was involved in a car accident. I spent five weeks in hospital in Dublin. I know now that my parents were worried about whether I would live or not. But when they were beside my bed, never once did I doubt that I wouldn't be going home. Their positive attitude got me through that dreadful period. My parents' love and determination won out. ← anecdote delivers the message

Patrick Kavanagh celebrates the wonders that we find in the most ordinary things, "wherever life pours ordinary plenty." This positive spirit should be an inspiration to us all. Thank you for listening this morning. My name is Cathy O'Rourke.

apt quotation

clear statement

EXERCISES

1. What qualities make this an effective radio talk? You should refer to both the content and the style of the talk.
2. Write the text of a speech that is to be broadcast on your favourite station on the subject: 'Listeners, spare a thought for Leaving Certificate students!'

   or

   Write out the text of a talk you might give on a radio show devoted to advice for Leaving Certificate students.

SUMMING UP COMPREHENDING B

Remember that the following steps are essential in these writing tasks:

1. Understanding the task.
2. Give attention to your:
   - AUDIENCE
   - LAYOUT/STRUCTURE
   - LANGUAGE
   - CONTENT
3. Draft and re-draft.
4. Ensure that your use of language is appropriate to the task.
5. Ensure that the finished version has a sense of completeness.

Notes

Notes

SECTION 4

COMPOSING

COMPOSITION

INTRODUCTION

REMEMBER: The composition question accounts for **25 per cent** of the overall grade in the Leaving Certificate English examination, so this is a particularly important chapter.

A **composition** is a substantial piece of writing. The most common compositions at Leaving Certificate level include the following:

- **Personal essay**
- **Talk/speech**
- **Article for newspapers/magazines**
- **Short story**
- **Descriptive essay**

You should practise writing compositions regularly to ensure that you feel confident doing one under exam conditions.

This section contains advice on how to write a composition. There are plenty of examples of the kinds of composition you will be expected to write for the Leaving Certificate examination.

- It is essential that the composition is your own work. With practice, you will find your own way of writing.
- The primary purpose of writing is to engage the reader, so make sure that you are original and have something interesting to write about.

How long?

A well-edited, tightly written piece of writing is more satisfying than a rambling, unfocused one. There is not a prescribed length for the composition, but an essay of between 700 and 900 words is definitely adequate. Time is better spent on structure and tightening expression than adding more pages. Your aim should be to complete the task set for you.

Good writing should:

- Be interesting.
- Show organisation and structure.
- Have something worthwhile to say.
- Avoid spelling errors.
- Be punctuated accurately.

- Use topic sentences.
- Develop paragraphs.
- Keep to the topic.
- Be original.
- Know its genre.
- Keep to its register.
- Have a rhythm.
- Please the reader.

Composing needs constant work and application.
Adapt your writing to a variety of tasks.

Does content really matter?

A composition is a *substantial* piece of writing, so you must do more than 'fill' four or five pages. Unless you have something worthwhile to say, your composition will be dull, and dull work will not receive many marks. Content matters a great deal.

For essays, articles and speeches that demand considerable content, you must spend time gathering ideas. A blank page will remain blank until you have something to write. There are a number of ways to get started.

PLANNING A COMPOSITION

1. BRAINSTORMING BY HEADINGS

This is a good method when the title requires you to discuss a topic.

For example, let us assume you are given the title, 'Why I Am Proud or Not Proud to be Irish'.

A series of **headings** can be used to help you gather ideas. Possibilities for such headings in this case are:

- political
- personal
- historical
- economic
- sport

The headings chosen will vary, obviously, depending upon the topic.

Each heading will generate a few ideas that will help you focus on the topic. Do not use the headings in your actual composition. On the right below, you can see some of the ideas that each heading has generated – these ideas can then be transformed into paragraphs and thoughtful content.

POLITICAL	Democracy/rich tradition/corruption/scandals/referenda
PERSONAL	A feeling of pride when abroad/anecdotes

HISTORICAL	Connection with ancient past/strong sense of independence/1916/Celts/Normans/ English/new wave of immigrants
ECONOMIC	Developed economy/social welfare
SPORT	GAA/international achievements/rugby/soccer/ Olympics

2. BRAINSTORMING BY SPIDOGRAM

Another method of brainstorming is through the use of a spidogram. In this case, you insert the essay title in the centre and link this to ideas generated on the theme. There can be several layers to your spidogram if necessary.

The example below, centred on the theme 'Proud to be Irish', can be added to using more arrows and circles.

STRUCTURE

It is essential that you properly structure your compositions. To use a cliché, it should have a **beginning**, **middle** and **end**.

INTRODUCTION

Make it clear to the reader what your central idea (thesis) is. The introduction can consist of an opening quotation/statement/anecdote followed by a short paragraph in which you set out your argument or main point. If possible, avoid a dull restatement of the question.

MAIN BODY

The body of the essay consists of well-structured paragraphs that use the points you have worked on in your plan. The more ideas you have, the better. Use plenty of supporting examples. Be coherent and consistent in your development of paragraphs. Seven or eight well-worked paragraphs will be sufficient.

CONCLUSION

Round off the composition with a clinching statement or quotation. Return to something you said at the beginning, but restate it in a slightly different manner, i.e. do not use the same words.

The composition should take the form of an arc. The reader should be left with a sense that your work is cohesive and complete.

Important Note

The above method is very useful for literature essays on Paper 2 where you have to respond to a specific question. Example:

- *"An audience responds to the protagonist in Shakespeare's tragedy with both sympathy and condemnation."* Discuss.

Here, you must respond to both elements referred to in the question.
In planning, you should gather material that will address:

- Why we should or should not have sympathy for the protagonist.
- Why he should or should not be condemned.

As you become more confident, you will be able to be more flexible in your approach.

Practice Exercise

Do the following to practise your skills at forming structures for essays.

Map out ideas for the following two compositions:

1. "Our education system needs a complete overhaul."
2. "Religion is still important in an age of technology."

Write out a structure for each.

EXPRESSION

How you express yourself is as important as what you say.

Establish a Clear and Appropriate Tone of VOICE

In an essay on literature, your tone should be neutral and objective. However, in a creative composition, you must establish a suitable tone. Do you want to come across as casual, personal, friendly or serious, persuasive? Remember, also, that humour can be a very useful means of communication and persuasion.

Remember:

- Getting your tone and register right are essential.
- Make sure your vocabulary is flexible and varied.

The examples that follow contain examples of students' work as well as the work of professional writers. It is hoped that they will encourage you to take your own writing seriously.

OFFICIAL CRITERIA OF ASSESSMENT FOR LEAVING CERTIFICATE ENGLISH (HIGHER LEVEL)

The tasks set for candidates in both Paper 1 and Paper 2 will be assessed in accordance with the following criteria:

• Clarity of Purpose (**P**) 30% of the marks.	• To display a clear and purposeful engagement with the set task.
• Coherence of Delivery (**C**) 30% of the marks.	• To sustain the response in an appropriate manner over the entire answer.
• Efficiency of Language Use (**L**) 30% of the marks.	• To manage and control language appropriate to the task.
• Accuracy of Mechanics (**M**) 10% of the marks.	• To display levels of accuracy in spelling and grammar appropriate to the required/ chosen register.

Notes

7

THE PERSONAL ESSAY

This is a substantial piece of writing in which you explore your attitudes to a particular subject.

It is important to strike the right tone in your writing. For example, you may wish to be serious or light-hearted, depending on your attitude to the subject and the relationship you want to establish with your reader.

Remember that although you are writing a personal essay, there is a reader who wants to be enlightened/entertained/engrossed by what you have to say. You must make sure that the quality of the writing is such that the reader will want to continue reading.

Avoid

- Telling a dull story.
- Filling pages with unnecessary/unfocused information.

Do

- Create a voice for yourself by establishing a definite tone.
- Convey something of your personality.
- Be honest (although there is room for creative exaggeration).

The **personal essay** explores a topic in a *personal* manner, i.e. it conveys your individual response to the topic or material. There are many ways that this can be done. Much depends on the topic you are writing about and your attitude to the topic, and the way you write about it. Writing about your family will require a different approach to a composition in which you address your attitude to the education system.

- As always, it is important to know what you are going to write before you begin, so **brainstorm** in order that you have plenty of ideas. **You must plan and structure your composition**.
- In order to make the content interesting and varied, you must know – and be seen to know – something about the topic. **Good compositions contain both information and opinion**.
- By the end of the composition, the reader should have some insight into you as a person. A measure of **reflection is important**, **as this demonstrates that you have thought about the topic**.

Getting started is the most difficult part of the writing process, which is why brainstorming and thoughtful planning are so important. Use your personal experience/books you read/films you have seen, and so on.

In the Leaving Certificate examination, the composition is the last question on Paper 1, so your mind will have been stimulated by a variety of texts and visual images by the time you reach it.

When writing a personal essay, you should do the following:

- Draw on your knowledge and experiences.
- Structure your ideas.
- Refer to books, articles, films, television programmes, and most importantly, your own personal experience.
- Offer reflection (considered original thoughts) on the topic.

Planning

Never begin a composition without devising a plan.

Read the following examples of personal writing. For each one, ask:

- How well does it address the task?
- Is the composition structured and coherent?
- How well has the writer used language?
- Are you are absorbed/interested/moved/entertained by the writing?

In each, take careful note of:

PURPOSE
STRUCTURE
EXPRESSION
CONTENT

In this personal essay, a Fifth-Year student, Pat Winston, explores the topic of dreams.

DREAMS

The ball swirls through the air and crashes into the roof of the net. One-nil. The ref whistles. *Champions!*

When I was young, I often played in the back garden. I would place the ball on the ground, stand back, close my eyes and wait for my imagination to take over. Slowly, the bushes became crowds, the swing a goal, and small buckets other players. When I opened them, I was in a World Cup final, taking a free kick on the edge of the area. Delight surged through me on scoring that goal.

We all dream. As a child, my dreams created other worlds to which I was able to escape at a whim. I would often be too busy saving the world from villains to hear my mum calling me down for dinner. It is strange to think that little pieces of plastic a few centimetres or so high, shaped like dinosaurs, could be taken as 100-foot monsters, but they were.

Now, looking at my little brother play with his Lego toys, I become jealous. On my desk are books and folders, assignments to complete and homework to do. Growing up changes the way we dream. I sometimes feel my mind wandering from a history essay. I wonder what grade I'll get. Then thoughts turn to what course I might end up doing in college. Suddenly, I see myself attending lectures, getting a degree and teaching. As I imagine walking into that first class... and then suddenly realise I have a five-page essay on Home Rule to do. The joy of day-dreaming comes at a price for a Leaving Cert student.

And yet dreams must be important. Why do we have them?

In the Bible, Joseph used dreams to tell the future. In the past, dreams were considered special, almost magical things. Some people believed it was the spirit world communicating with us. Only gifted people could find the meaning of dreams. Dreams contained special messages.

More recently, the psychologist Freud discovered that dreams could tell us about our secrets. He seated his patients on a couch and asked them to recall their dreams. These revealed their deepest concerns. A world hidden from view was opened up and a new branch of medicine was born.

A while ago, I was chatting with mum and she told me she still often dreams of sitting her Leaving. Her dream always begins in an examination hall. The papers are being handed out. It is geography. Then, an announcement is made: "You have fifteen minutes left." She panics. Suddenly, the scene changes and she is on a beach and the tide is coming in over the sand. Her desk is being lapped by waves. She cannot finish her exam. At this point, she wakes up.

Mum told me that dreams like this are called anxiety dreams. Maybe her unconscious mind is telling her that she is stressed about something. As she actually did well in geography, the message might be that there is nothing to worry about. Knowing this, she says, makes her feel better.

Sometimes, people have dreams that predict the future. I read about a woman who dreamt about a plane crash. She was due to go on holiday the next day but was too frightened to get on the plane because of her dream. The plane crashed and everybody on board was killed. Maybe dreams are like a sixth sense.

Dreams can be important to us in very practical ways. They can motivate you to aim for what seems impossible. You hear people on television saying things like: *My dream is to play for United* or *my dream is open my own restaurant* or *mine is to be a famous singer.* If you have a special dream in life, you might then work hard to see if the dream can come true. I think these kinds of dreams can be good if the people have some talent. Too often, though, real losers appear on telly with no talent at all, just a silly dream.

It was my dream to be on the local under-16 hurling team. I practised every day and finally I was a sub. In the semi-final, the full forward got injured. All my training paid off because I had to play. Although I was on for only twenty minutes, it was one of the best moments of my life.

I want to go to university. At the moment, that is my dream. I am studying hard. The dream of being a sports instructor or a history teacher keeps me focused. This dream is a far cry from my childhood dream of playing in a World Cup final. This one is attainable.

Another interesting thing about dreams is that your mind works in a different way when you are dreaming. I remember a few months ago I was grappling with a particularly difficult maths problem. I stayed up until after twelve trying to solve it. I gave up. Amazingly, when I woke up the next morning I knew the answer. Was my unconscious mind working on the problem while I slept? Many scientists have claimed to have made startling discoveries in their sleep.

John Lennon the famous singer, and ex-Beatle, said in the song 'Imagine':

Imagine there's no countries
It isn't hard to do
Nothing to kill or die for
And no religion too
Imagine all the people
Living life in peace.

That was his dream. The song has inspired many people. It is a dream we could all do well to try to make come true. Maybe it is as unrealistic as my childish dream of being a World Cup winner. But wouldn't life be dull without such dreams?

EXERCISES

1. Consider your own response to this essay. Does it succeed as a personal essay?
2. Does it have the following?
   - Clarity of purpose yes / no
   - Coherence of delivery yes / no
   - Language of expression yes / no
3. How will studying this piece help to improve your own writing?
4. Mark it out of 100.
5. Write a personal essay on the importance of dreams in your life.

TEXT 2

In the following composition, a Sixth-Year student, Grainne Sheil, writes on things that annoy her.

THINGS THAT ANNOY ME

Where to start? Ever since I was a little girl, I have been irritated very easily. At home, it doesn't take much to set me off on a rant, which usually ends with, "Stop, or I am telling mum!" I know, very mature for a girl a few weeks before her 18th birthday.

My list is endless: know-it-alls, spam mail, the bus fare increase from 80 to 85 cent (there is a huge difference, you know), grinding teeth, family outings, being a tourist in another country, looking like a tourist in another country, the Irish weather, my principal, waiting, boys with greasy hair, men with none, people who slurp their drinks, being the eldest in a family of three girls, people cracking their bones, messy eaters, loud chewers, spiders, cleaning out the goldfish tank, parents...I could go on.

One thing, however, that I have not mentioned, is so annoying that it requires an entire list to itself: the Leaving Cert. Studying the flowering plant; the composition of eggs; the subjunctive in French; the never-ending pressure; the constant reading; studying; note-taking. It's just all getting too much.

A place where I have been spending much of my time this year is the library (I find it impossible to study at home – too many annoying distractions!). Librarians are a breed of people apart. They are quite possibly the most suspicious, power-driven, finicky, annoying people I have ever encountered. *"Five minutes left on the Internet", "No, you need valid ID to take out this book", "Are you aware you owe quite a substantial amount of money here?", "No talking, eating, drinking, or listening to CD players in this library", "Actually try not to breathe in here, we prefer the dead."* Do librarians have friends or family? Do they socialise only with each other? Probably. I can't imagine them ever having a fun night out with normal people.

And yet the library is heaven compared to home. Imagine trying to concentrate on suicidal poets, trigonometry and the Land Acts, with the theme tune of Coronation Street, bickering siblings and stressed-out parents all blaring in the background.

Upon reading the title of this essay, a boy I went out with last year sprung to mind. Hugh was his name. Hugh was the definition of 'perfect'. Hugh excelled at school, was the captain of the rugby team, had a wide circle of friends and was amazingly good-looking. When Hugh and I began to see each other, I was delighted. Everything was brilliant (I was fantasising about the church, the honeymoon, the pets running around our immense garden), until we went out for dinner. Hugh had absolutely appalling table manners. After slurping his way through the broccoli and pumpkin soup, he proceeded to shovel his way through the main course, while telling me about his mates. Each sentence was finished with yet another shovelful of food into an already full mouth. I was horrified. From that moment on, I realised that this 'perfect guy' was not all that perfect and the small things he did after that became immense barriers to our relationship. His sniffling, nail-biting, walking with his two feet slightly inverted, began to gnaw at my soul. Needless to say, I broke up with him within a week.

My school is extremely old as well as extremely extensive. Because of this, it is impossible to get to each class on time. There are several corridors I have still never been down; it's like Hogwart's without the magic. Well, my punctuality, or lack of, does not go unnoticed. Because of this I am a regular attendee at Saturday morning detention. This means getting up at half six. Each week I am met by a cantankerous hung-over teacher, who outlines the task. It usually involves scraping chewing gum from the tables and chairs. Chewing gum (another for my annoying list) is banned in my school. This prohibition only makes it more thrilling for students to indulge in. Why don't teachers learn that rules are to be broken? Remove the rule and you remove the problem.

Well, from reading this I probably come across as a narky, easily annoyed teenager who does not appreciate what she has (by the way I hate the way adults always say we don't know how fortunate we are). But you see, it is really the small things that annoy me. One being the fact that the ink in cartridge pens is always running ou....

EXERCISES

1. Consider your own response to this essay. Does it succeed as a personal essay?
2. Does it have the following?
   - Clarity of purpose yes / no
   - Coherence of delivery yes / no
   - Language of expression yes / no
3. How will studying this piece help to improve your own writing?
4. Mark it out of 100.
5. Write a personal essay on the things that annoy you.

TEXT 3

In this personal composition, John Ryan writes on the topic of relationships that matter to him.

A RELATIONSHIP THAT IS IMPORTANT TO ME

"What's this, Dad?"

"Where did you find it? That's an old Horslips album. I haven't listened to that in years."

Little did I think that a search in the attic for a suitcase to use on my Transition school trip to Rome would result in a history lesson on '70's music and the beginning of a wonderful relationship with my dad. Until that day, he was someone who I didn't really know. That afternoon, we ransacked the attic for more "great music". He even hauled down an old record player and explained how a needle digging into a revolving disc (album/vinyl) could produce amazing sounds: "Nothing like your soulless MP3 players and iPods."

What astounded me was how seriously and passionately he was into his music. He caressed the surface of each vinyl disc with a cloth before gently easing it onto the record player.

Since that fateful day, he has retrieved all his albums from the attic and they are now alphabetically arranged in the sitting room (Mum is threatening divorce) and every so often the family is rocked by the incredible guitar solos of Led Zeppelin or Black Sabbath or the poetry of Dylan and the weirdly wonderful Bowie.

In the last two years, something has happened to me. I have stopped being embarrassed by my dad and his music (although the photos of him in flared jeans and wearing hair down his shoulders is really something that freaks me out. *Great music Dad, but you looked creepy!*).

During the Christmas holidays, when I was in 5th year, he took me to the Horslips reunion gig at the Point. Suddenly, all the barriers between the generations came crashing down as we both were transported to that special place where music exists. We bopped and head-banged (and air-guitared) to the soaring guitar of Johnny Fean ("an Irish Hendrix" according to dad).

What is amazing is that up until our musical odyssey, we never really bonded at all. Dad had tried to get me interested in his other passion (football) and in particular (and very sadly) Leeds United. He signed me up for the local under-eights but gave up when I was an eternal sub. Once, I managed to get on the starting team (when illness decimated the team), but was humiliated by being substituted and no one brought on to replace me. The coach correctly reckoned that 10 players would do better than a full team with me. That is when Dad gave up on me as a player. As for supporting Leeds, I never saw the point. The other kids in school at least could celebrate success with Man United and Chelsea. Most had never heard of Leeds. From that time, I was happy with Nintendo and Dad became an invisible presence. If I needed help with homework, I went to Mum. A note to excuse me, I went to Mum. Pocket money, again Mum.

Throughout my early teens, I considered my dad to be a grumpy, intolerant and opinionated dinosaur. According to him: MTV was crap; *The X-Factor* useless moronic crap; rap was crap. I just thought he hated music. In the car, he always had the radio tuned into *Morning Ireland* (or is that *Moaning Ireland*?) and George Hook and endless talk. At least at home we had two TVs. He could enjoy his Champion League action, *Match of the Day*, and endless crime dramas, while I enjoyed re-runs of *Father Ted*, *Scrubs* and (mindless) reality-TV shows. We inhabited parallel worlds.

That day of my discovery of his musical treasure-trove in the attic changed everything. A line of communication opened up. He educated me on what music was and I even got him into Coldplay. We connected.

> I used to rule the world,
> Seas would rise when I gave the world,
> Now in the morning I sleep alone,
> Sweep the streets I used to own.

This song, along with Eminem's *Stan*, are now on his car mix favourites. We no longer have to suffer car journeys with the radio droning with sad voices of people "talking to Joe". Talk Radio has been replaced by *Talking Heads*, a great band of the late '70s. We both agree that the *X-Factor* is crap but Simon Cowell can be a good laugh. We agree that music was great in the past but there is still great stuff being written today. He has moved forward and I have stepped back in time, and magically we have met up.

Music has cemented a great father-son relationship. We feel a bit sad for Mum who thinks Jedward are cute, that Elton John is great and that music should never be too loud.

EXERCISES

1. Consider your own response to this essay. Does it succeed as a personal essay?
2. Does it have the following?
   - Clarity of purpose yes / no
   - Coherence of delivery yes / no
   - Language of expression yes / no
3. How will studying this piece help to improve your own writing?
4. Mark it out of 100.
5. Write a personal essay on family life.

TEXT 4

Asked to write a personal essay on an aspect of the education system, Michael Lockhart, a Sixth-Year student, wrote a light-hearted, informal essay on mathematics.

LONG LIVE MATHS!

We've heard it all before: "Maths is visible in every aspect of our daily lives. We use maths when we get out of bed. We use it when we go school. We use it in school (particularly in maths class)." And so on. We seem to use maths in absolutely everything. "It allows us to build cars, roads, houses, schools, hospitals, trains, aeroplanes...modern civilisation is built on numbers. We couldn't survive without maths."

This, at least, is what my maths teacher would say. During a particularly tedious lesson on (far too) complex numbers, I decided to disprove this incessant waffle on the wonders of maths...I would try to get through a single day without using maths.

Well, at least that was my original plan. I soon changed my mind when I realised I wouldn't be able to use the DART that day, and would have to walk the fifteen miles between my house and school. I'd be happy in the knowledge that I was pushing the boundaries of science, or at least trying to topple them over in an explosion of numbers, but laziness overcame my desire to prove by experiment that maths isn't necessary. I would have to be content with imagining this maths-free day. That night, I lay down on my bed, closed my eyes and drifted off to a place where 'sin' meant simply an offence against God and 'tan' was just a darkening of the skin...

I would eventually be woken by the cacophony of bird-cries outside my window. No alarm clocks for me, with their eerily green numbers glaring at me from my desk. I'd leave ample time to make myself breakfast, get dressed and walk to school. It would be a long, arduous walk. I'd sing to myself on the way. After all, who needs iPods?

I'd eventually arrive at school, probably quite late (though I would have no way of knowing). I'd head to first class vaguely wondering if it was over yet.

While thinking about this no-maths day, I was delighted to discover that we don't use it much in school. Apart from the electronic bells and the (overused) computers, most subjects could get along very nicely with chalk and talk and, of course, clay tablets. That must be ironic.

Without maths, the buildings would be crooked, the stairs would be dangerous and the elevators would be like a ride from Disneyland (though probably not as fun, and definitely not as safe). Oh, and the lights wouldn't work...or electricity in general. My point is we could get by. Plus, we'd have at least one less class in the day.

After a morning of stumbling across uneven floors, tripping on tilting staircases and guessing when each class would end, I'd sit down for lunch.

Food is another thing that doesn't need maths. Obviously, packaged foods filled with identically shaped snacks couldn't exist, but they're hardly essential. There would be no chocolate bar or soft drink dispensers. I'd munch away happily on my apple, staring out through the blurry misshapen window, as algebra became a distant memory.

The afternoon would be much the same as the morning, except that the sun's slow descent would reduce visibility in the dim corridors. After a few bumps into my fellow students, and some minor tumbles down the stairs, I'd head home.

The return journey would be slightly more difficult than the morning trip. The darkness would make navigating the pot-holed, bumpy pathways and roads a nightmare, but at least there would be no cars to worry about.

I'd arrive at my poorly built, lopsided house late at night. I'd stagger through the ill-proportioned door and make my way slowly up the stairs. Homework would not be an option: the lack of light would make finding my desk challenging, let alone writing an Irish essay. I'd sit down in my room, twiddling my thumbs, and then eventually drift down the stairs for dinner.

The lack of a gas or electric oven would make cooking a long and tedious process. I'd have to start a fire, and without a television I wouldn't have learnt how to do this from Bear Grylls. Eventually, I'd manage, and I'd cook whatever food we had in the house that hadn't gone off. There would be no freezers or fridges in this maths-free world.

After this (probably burnt) meal, I'd go to bed. There'd little else to do in this all-engulfing darkness. I'd fall into a deep sleep, nursing my bruised limbs and weary feet, and waiting for the dawn chorus to announce the beginning of a new day.

I opened my eyes. Then I laughed in triumph. I'd done it! I'd survived a day without using maths! Well, I had imagined surviving a day without maths, but had proved a point. Maths is not essential to survival – technically speaking, at least.

I don't expect this little experiment of mine to change things, except maybe thin the smile on my maths' teacher's face, and I don't really want to change things anyhow. Proving that maths is not essential doesn't mean I want it gone.

In the long run, I think, spending forty minutes a day sitting in a classroom enduring yet another tedious lesson on trigonometry is preferable to living like an Ewok.

We don't need maths to survive, but we do need it to be comfortable. My inspirational step towards reducing our dependence on science will go unheeded… Maths will live on.

EXERCISES

1. Consider your own response to this essay. Does it succeed as a personal essay?
2. Does it have the following?
   - Clarity of purpose yes / no
   - Coherence of delivery yes / no
   - Language of expression yes / no
3. How will studying this piece help to improve your own writing?
4. Mark it out of 100.
5. Write a personal essay on your experience of a school subject.

TEXT 5

In this extract from his autobiography Moab is my Washpot, *the writer and television broadcaster Stephen Fry describes his experience of being sent to boarding school at seven.*

ON BOARDING AT PUBLIC SCHOOL

When people today hear that I was sent away to board at a school two hundred miles from home at the age of seven they often raise a disapproving eyebrow, snort a contemptuous snort or fling up a despairing hand at the coldness, cruelty and neglect of parents who could do such a thing to a child of such tender years: the words "bosom" and "snatching" and phrases like "how could any ...?" and "at such an age" and "no wonder the British are so..." are often used.

There is great stupidity in this reaction, or at least minimal imagination, which is more or less the same thing, but morally worse. What is forgotten by those who dislike the idea of children being sent away at an early (or any) age is the matter of expectation and custom. The rightness or wrongness of private boarding education is a separate issue and I change my opinion about it as regularly as I change my socks, the desktop pattern on my computer screen and my views on God.

When I was seven years old every child I knew of my own age went away to boarding school. Again the rightness or wrongness of being friendly only with children from similar backgrounds is a separate issue. The point is that my father had been to boarding school, my mother had been to boarding school, all the friends I had in the world went away to boarding school. It was what one did. It was Life as I knew it. A child of seven does not question such circumstance: it is the way of the world. If I had *not* been sent away I should have wondered what was wrong with me. I should have felt neglected and left out. At a local day school I most emphatically should *not* have felt more loved or more cared for, far from it. Going round to play with friends in the school holidays and listening to their stories of boarding school would have left me feeling miserably excluded and inexplicably singled out for strange and unusual treatment. I know this for a fact, for I did spend a term at a primary school and, sweet and friendly as the place was, I couldn't wait to leave and join my brother at boarding school.

Had we lived in Central London I dare say it might have been different. As it was we were hidden in the mysterious interior of East Anglia, where the nearest shop was a twenty-minute bicycle ride away and the nearest friends many miles farther. There was no door-bell ringing and *can-Stephen-come-out-to-play-ing* in Booton, Norfolk: no cool friends called Zak and Barnaby and Luke, no parks, no Saturday morning cinema clubs, no milk-shake parlours, no buses, no visiting ice-cream vans, no roller-skating rinks. When city-bred friends saw the house I lived in, they cooed with envy and delight at the idea of so much space with so much nature all around. I used to coo with envy when I stayed in a terraced house in suburban London and saw fitted carpets, central heating and drawing-rooms that were called sitting-rooms and had televisions in them.

It is also true that the ineptly hidden distress of my mother at the end of the school holidays gave me more direct, clear testament of absolute love than most children are ever lucky enough to receive at such an early age. Private education may be a divisive abomination, it may leave its product weird and ridiculous in all kinds of insanitary and peculiar ways, it may have held back the social development of this country, it may be responsible for all kinds of disasters and unpleasantness, but in my case it never left me feeling starved of parental love and attention. Whether at boarding school, day school or at home with governesses and private tutors, I would always have been as screwed up as an unwanted letter from the *Reader's Digest*. Wherever I have been, whatever I have done, I should have experienced an adolescence of *Sturm*, *Drang*, disaster and embarrassment.

EXERCISES

1. Consider your own response to this essay. Does it succeed as a personal essay?
2. Does it have the following?
   - Clarity of purpose yes / no
   - Coherence of delivery yes / no
   - Language of expression yes / no
3. How will studying this piece help to improve your own writing?
4. Mark it out of 100.
5. Write a personal essay on your experience of childhood friends.

8

THE SPEECH

The personal essay is a flexible kind of writing. However, when you are delivering a speech, you have a more direct relationship with your audience. This must be obvious from the way that you communicate.

In writing and delivering a speech, you must:

- **Establish a relationship with audience.**
- **Have a clear purpose in giving the speech.**
- **Present your material in a way that is interesting.**

PLANNING IS ESSENTIAL

FORMAL DEBATE

A speech for a formal debate must persuade an audience. A motion is presented and you must argue 'for' or 'against' the motion. The task is to convince listeners.

The formalities:

- Introduce yourself to your audience: "Ladies and gentlemen of the house, adjudicators, members of the opposition, fellow team mates and, of course, chairman..."
- Define the motion and address it.
- Address the audience. Keep them interested.
- Reinforce your argument.
- Use plenty of examples.
- Offer a strong conclusion.

Language

Speak to your audience: use repetition and rhetorical questions.
Use reason and logic to make inferences.

A weak argument will:

- Be poorly supported.
- Be poorly reasoned.
- Be inconsistent and contradictory.
- Be full of generalisations.
- Have no sense of the audience.
- Be disjointed.
- Have careless spelling and punctuation.
- Have poor paragraphing.

A strong argument will:

- Have a central argument or thesis.
- Use relevant examples.
- Have a sense of the audience.
- Use persuasive language.
- Be coherently structured.

TEXT 1

The following speech was written by a Sixth-Year student, Maria Tyrell. The motion of the school debate was "Women are the inferior sex" and the students were asked to write a speech either 'for' or 'against' the motion.

THE TRUE 'INFERIOR SEX'

Many civilisations have been destroyed by wars. Who has been responsible for this destruction? Men.

Ladies and gentlemen of the house, adjudicators, members of the opposition and, of course, chairman, I am putting it to you, that men are destructive, violent and inferior. If our civilisation is to survive, the superior sex must exert more influence. The evidence of women's superiority is all around us. I firmly oppose the motion that women are inferior.

While our male politicians are involved in scandal after scandal, who are the public figures that have gained most respect? Some come to mind immediately – Mary McAleese and Mary Robinson at home and figures like Angela Merkel abroad. Who is the biggest selling author today? J.K. Rowling. A woman. In the Leaving Certificate, who performs better? Girls. Members

of the house, you cannot deny the evidence.

Yes, in the past, women played a less successful role in society. But why? Because men ruled and ruled badly. The twentieth century was a century of war and bloodshed. Where were the women in all of this? Certainly not fighting. Certainly not sending people to fight. No. Women were kept at home. Women dressed men's wounds and looked after families abandoned by men who went off to kill. You might remind me that many armies in our developed world now have women soldiers. But this only proves that men want to spread the pain of their sick civilisation.

Imagine for a moment an end of term school report for the respective achievements of men and women. How well would men do?

In maths: fail. For needlessly subtracting millions from the world's population through warfare.

In religion: fail. For causing division and strife, and for excluding women from any role in the hierarchy of religious institutions. Look at the popes, bishops, Dali Lamas, ayatollahs, priests. All men.

In history: fail. Man has never learnt anything from history. He has continued to repeat the mistakes of the past.

In science: another fail. Each invention has been used to kill, destroy and harm. Didn't Oppenheimer disown his achievement in working on the atom when he saw its destructive use.

Economics: I don't have to prove anything to you. Man's economics have ruined most economies.

If this house judges us on human qualities, you will certainly agree that women are superior. So, an end of school report for women might be as follows. Maths: an A for increasing the population through childbirth and keeping people alive through caring. History: an A for learning from man's mistakes. We will not mistreat you. Languages: an A for being better communicators than men.

In the few short years since being liberated from men, women have overtaken them in many places. In our schools and universities, girls and young women are doing better academically. The statistics are there to prove it. Girls are better at studying. Boys are easily distracted. Teachers in the audience, I put a question to you: who would you rather teach?

However, if you are not convinced by what I have said so far, then my next argument is irrefutable. Boys, you are redundant! You will soon no longer be needed in reproduction. With cloning, it is the woman who contains the important chromosomes – not men. We could soon have a society like bees. In a beehive, the queen is happy to have millions of male workers for her entertainment. But don't worry, as the superior sex, we will not mistreat you as women have been mistreated for thousands of years. No, we are kinder and more civilised than you are.

Where is the proof? As mothers, wives, and nurses, women have always displayed more love and compassion than men. That is why when wars were being fought, women became nurses to heal and look after men.

I put it to this house that we are superior in every way except one. In the past, men used their physical strength as proof of superiority. Yes, men can lift heavy weights. So what? So can an ox! Yes, men can run faster, but so can a cheetah! Ladies and gentlemen, the things that men can do better than women are things animals can do. We prove our superiority in being better humans.

Members of the house, if civilisation is to flourish, it will be because we women will finally be allowed to demonstrate our superiority.

EXERCISES

1. Consider your own response to this speech. Does it convince you?
2. Does it have the following?
   - Clarity of purpose yes / no
   - Coherence of delivery yes / no
   - Language of expression yes / no
3. How will studying this piece help to improve your own writing?
4. Mark it out of 100.
5. Write a speech (either 'for' or 'against') on the topic, "This society does not treat its people in a fair way".

TEXT 2

The following speech was written by Eoin Healy, a Sixth-Year student, in response to the motion, "This house thinks that it is important to preserve our national culture and identity."

CULTURE AND IDENTITY

Good evening ladies and gentlemen, I would like to take this opportunity to welcome you all here this evening as we debate the motion that it is "important to preserve our national culture and identity." I truly believe that the imminent death of our unique Irish cultural identity is a pressing issue. It is all too easy to ignore the matter as we go about our daily lives. Over the next few minutes, I hope to convince you that we (and many peoples throughout the world) should do our utmost to preserve who and what we are.

In by-gone days, nations did not have to work hard to maintain their individuality. Lack of transport kept each separate culture safe from outside influence and generally ignorant of other ways of life. Humans across the globe spoke different languages, worshipped different gods, constructed things differently, wore different clothes and had different customs. Egyptians had their pyramids, the Babylonians their renowned gardens, the Chinese their wall, and Vikings their longboats and hilarious horned helmets. Today, if one was to ask what Ireland is famous for, the common answer would probably be drink and, maybe, potatoes. Is this not deeply worrying?

In the early 1900s, the Wright Brothers developed the airplane and suddenly the world became a smaller place. During the next hundred years, developments in communication and information technologies further shrunk this planet, making it into a global village. One terrible consequence of all of this has been the obliteration of vulnerable cultures.

After World War Two, multinationals came into existence. McDonalds, Nike, IBM, Coca-Cola, and a host of others have colonised the planet with their goods. While our grandparents might have sipped a quaint lemonade made in a local factory, today we in Ireland drink millions of gallons of carbonated cola. The global market has become a tide, a tsunami if you wish, which has drowned small local enterprise.

Today, we flock to the commercial Mecca that is Dundrum and purchase the same goods as our peers in New York and London. The international High Street has replaced the local shop.

In the 1960s, media corporations put satellites into space that could transmit signals from all around the world. While this united the population of Earth, as it tuned into the famous Moon landing in 1969, its effect has been catastrophic for local cultures. American television culture has become ours. You only have to listen, as you travel by DART or shop in Dundrum, to the accents and the language of Irish young people. "Oh my God!" or "OMG!" is heard everywhere in voices straight out of American TV. We are no longer influenced by our rich heritage. Instead, we get our language from American rap and Hollywood movies. Even that word ('movies') seems to have replaced the 'pictures' that my parents still use. Hasn't our Irishness been diluted?

In the late '80s, personal computers and the Internet were pioneered by Bill Gates and Steve Jobs. The world became even smaller again. Of course, this is a plus for families struck by the disaster of emigration; however, it has struck the death-knell for national culture. The things that defined cultures have faded. Nations have given up what makes them unique.

In cultural terms, there has been a victor. The United States. We speak its version of English, listen to its music and eat its food, watch its movies. Even our greatest cultural success, U2, is really an American band. They are not renowned for their jigs and reels, are they? The other great global power in cultural terms is Britain. Football and rugby are the games that have captured the world's attention. They both originated on the soil of our next-door neighbour. Go out into the schools of Ireland and you will see jerseys with the colours of Man United, Liverpool, Celtic. And if you listen to us talk in the corridors before school on Monday, the chances are the conversation will turn to *The X-Factor* at some stage.

My point, ladies and gentlemen, is that our national culture has been choked to a near-death. We speak the language, we wear the clothes, have the same cultural pursuits of our American and British colonisers. Isn't it quite ironic that after winning our independence, we have given it up so easily? In the years since 1922, have we become less Irish? Haven't we embraced cultural pursuits that do not have their origins in our Gaelic past?

Why is it necessary then to try to preserve our own national identity? What has it done for us? Isn't this global culture not better than what we had? I can only say that without a culture that is ours, we are nothing. A mere cog in a machine. A group of people that will leave nothing to those that come after us: a people who will not have a legacy. Are we heading to a future similar to the one mapped out by Orwell in his novel *1984*? One in which the past was wiped out.

Don't get me wrong, ladies and gentlemen: I am not an anti-capitalist, say-no-to-globalisation, conspiracy theorist who sees deep plots in everything. I am not a believer in turning back the clock and trying to live by the code of the ancient Fianna. I am not a nut job. In fact, I welcome many changes that technology has brought. I am comfortable with my Playstation and iPod. I am delighted that televised shots of famines in Africa can be beamed around the world, raising consciousness, and helping to highlight global poverty. I am delighted that new technologies can empower people. We have seen revolutions ousting tyrannical regimes and these uprisings have been aided by Twitter, Facebook, text-messaging and the Internet. Information technology is a good thing, in most respects.

My argument is that our cultural identity is worth preserving and this is made very difficult in the world we live in. I think we, you listening tonight and me, have a huge task to undertake. A burden lies upon our shoulders. We have a mission to perform. We must not let our heritage, our culture, history, language, myths and legends, be forgotten. If we do, we will become imitation Americans; or second-rate British. Joyce and Beckett, Wilde and Yeats, O'Casey and Heaney – these have demonstrated their Irishness on the world stage. We must be proud of who we are and we must first know who we are. Sadly, we seem to be forgetting our past as we move into the future. The battle to be fought is with ourselves. Our culture will be preserved if we want it badly enough. The depressing fact is that it might be too late.

Ladies and gentlemen, I believe our culture is worth preserving. I hope you do also.

EXERCISES

1. Consider your own response to this speech. Does it convince you?
2. Does it have the following?
   - Clarity of purpose yes / no
   - Coherence of delivery yes / no
   - Language of expression yes / no
3. How will studying this piece help to improve your own writing?
4. Mark it out of 100.
5. Write a speech addressing the motion "Ireland is still a great place in which to live." You can argue for or against.

THE ARTICLE

INTRODUCTION

An article is a lengthy piece of prose, generally produced for a magazine or newspaper. When writing an article, you must take into account the publication and its readership. Ask yourself the following questions:

1. **What is the purpose of the article?**

   An **informative article** will contain facts, e.g. an article on jobs and young people.

   In contrast, a **persuasive article** will try to peddle an idea, e.g. an article aimed at persuading your readers of the benefits of computer literacy.

2. **Who is the audience?**

   The publication and subject matter of the article will determine your audience, e.g. a Sunday newspaper, magazine and school yearbook will each have different audiences.

3. **How is it going to be structured?**

   The introduction and conclusion should be given special attention. You should also take care with paragraphs and topic sentences.

4. **What register will be employed?**

   Your relationship with your audience and your topic will determine whether you will adopt a formal or informal approach. Articles tend to be more personal than reports. There is room for opinion and the expression of your point of view.

WRITING THE ARTICLE

An article must be suited to the magazine/newspaper and the particular readership. What is your brief? What have you been asked to do?

There can be a personal element in an article, but it is not just a personal reflection.

Whether you are providing information, being persuasive, or giving a personal view, will depend on what you have been asked to do.

For example, the three requests below will result in three completely different kinds of article:

- Write an article on the experience of moving house.
- Write an article in which you persuade readers that the education system is outdated.
- Write a humorous article on the trials and tribulations of school trips.

Here are some basic tips on writing an article:

- Hook the reader with an interesting opening paragraph.
- Show that you have structured your article.
- The writing should be fluid.
- The content should hold the reader's attention.
- There should be interesting turns of phrase.
- There should be no needless repetition.
- Establish a definite tone (either serious/ironic/humorous).
- The conclusion should round off the article and leave the reader with something to think about.

When you read your first draft, you should check that the above points are covered. Read it over to hear what sounds awkward.

TEXT 1

In the following article, two Fifth-Year students, Eugene Egan and Rory Crean, have been asked to submit two articles outlining their response to the view that "Religion has a role to play in schools."

RELIGION IN SCHOOLS

Eugene Egan AGREES

It is underestimated just how quickly the world is changing. Twenty years ago the bulk of the world's information was stored in books – in cold, hard text, collected *en masse* in (now antiquated) repositories known as 'libraries'. Now, staggering amounts of information can be stored in a chip the size of a fingernail. Ten years ago, a mobile phone was a clunky, oversized brick that had the sound quality of a cassette covered in sand and emitted gamma radiation; now, it's scarcely bigger than a pack of cards. Just a few short years ago, none of these comparisons were clichéd.

And as a kind of side-effect to this exponential advancement in technology, there's a growing feeling within the current generation that any progress is good progress. This is why, for example, DVDs are being replaced by Blue-Ray discs. Change for the sake of it, for the sake of a minor thrill that puffs out of existence once you realise that things haven't changed, and may in fact be a little worse. If I buy a Blue-Ray player instead of a DVD player, the movies will cost on average a fiver more than a regular DVD, and over time it's going to add up. If you don't allow the teaching of religion in schools, you end up with kids who might be perfectly passable in everyday life, but don't have any kind of moral backbone.

Get ready to spit out the beverage you are drinking in disbelieving disbelief, because here it comes: religion is inherently good. When followed dogmatically and without reason, then it is bad. When the trust that comes as part of being a professor of that religion is abused, then it is bad. But the idea of religion – a code of ethics by which to live one's life – is an entirely good one. It is completely and utterly up to the individual to decide what he or she believes. But to presume that that individual will arrive at a reasonable and compassionate moral code (as offered by the major world religions that are taught in schools throughout the world) on their own, when other outside influences are almost guaranteed to be unsavory in some sense, is naïve to say the least. It's wise to have a guiding touch, however light.

But to get to the crux of this argument, why should it be up to the schools to enforce this? Because, quite simply, for the last however-many-thousands-of-years, religion was taught at home. Then along came a few wandering visionaries who decreed that all children should receive an education; whenceforth, we were whisked away from home and plonked into school. School, not home, is now where we spend the majority of our day. And when we get home, no one is going to waste time taking you through the various Hindu prayers for when food is prepared or the more intricate and subtle points of Islamic laws governing Ramadan or the finer points of Christian doctrine – though it seems that a lot of people feel someone should. So, it's schools which step into the breach.

It is not the job of the Board/Department/Ministry or whatever of Education, or schools, or teachers to tell a student what to believe. And luckily enough, in practice the teachers and Department of Education agree with this. They lay out a buffet of religious ideas for us to flavor. Those ideas we like, we will usually take to heart (and soul). We are not force fed. The final decision is with us but at least we have been offered a choice.

Rory Crean DISAGREES

I am a Catholic, that is to say that I was born into a Catholic family, educated in a Catholic school and I was taught one religion…so I picked it. Personally, I believe that had I been born as the same person but in a different family, or educated in a different religious school, I would not be of the same religion. An article published in the *Irish Times* at the time of writing reported on the comments of Gordon Linney, a retired Archdeacon of the Church of Ireland, stating that, while the education system did need reform, it should not be "on terms dictated by a secular agenda."

I could not disagree more. Religion is fast becoming obsolete. Its presence in modern society is almost non-existent. In the workplace, religious symbols are discouraged if not banned completely, so why, then, should schools be any different? What is school life if not preparation for one's working life? While the compulsory course I took during the Junior Cert did teach me the basics of the world religions, I sincerely doubt that without that knowledge I would have landed myself in a religious *faux-pas* of epic proportions.

Throughout my Primary and Secondary school education, I was taught about Jesus, Jesus's friends, Jesus's miracles, and how Jesus was an all round pretty stand-up guy. And, at the end of all of that, I was welcomed/accepted/ forced into Catholicism. While I'm not rejecting my religion, I certainly feel that an element of personal choice was removed from me, and that's what is important. Personal choice is becoming a larger factor in how young people mature and without a sense of autonomy in terms of religious choice, and any other major life decision for that matter, a young person's maturing process is somewhat damaged. Having a religion imposed on you is an odd thing. I didn't suddenly inherit any kind of prejudice; I wasn't forced to accept things that were against my moral code; religion did me no irreparable harm. All I had from it was a definite answer to a question I never asked: What religion are you?

If you and your family come to the decision to believe in a set of dogmas and wish to commit to them, then fire away and attend whatever services you wish, and partake in whatever rites you must, in order to prove your commitment, but religion should not be dragged into school life, and students' lives. School is for teaching children skills and giving them knowledge for their lives as adults.

For me, keeping religion in schools is hypocritical. It's not as if without religion we'd all be impolite, inconsiderate people. Morality and religion aren't two sides of the same coin; they're two coins in the same currency. Schools are bringing a discriminating factor into students' lives. By making religion an educational subject, difference between students is highlighted and this results in two problems: it either means many different schools must be established to cater for these different religions, thus keeping children separate; or it creates religious tension within one school where students of different religions attend. Either way, religion in school does not lead to social cohesion. Would Northern Irish children have benefitted from being educated together without religion in schools?

Practise what you preach. Our schools are supposed to create free and autonomous citizens. If schools took that advice to heart all forms of discrimination and separateness would be removed from schools. That includes religion. By doing so, schools would become a neutral environment, their focus primarily on producing mature students who are ready to take their place in society. Let's leave teaching to teachers in schools and preaching to preachers – outside.

NOTES

MY RESPONSE TO THE ARTICLE:	
CLARITY OF PURPOSE:	
COHERENCE OF DELIVERY:	
LANGUAGE OF EXPRESSION:	
HOW WILL THESE HELP ME TO IMPROVE MY OWN WRITING:	
MARK OUT OF 100:	

EXERCISES

Write an article on ONE of the following topics:

1. Write an article for a national newspaper on the topic: "The Leaving Certificate course offers Irish students a balanced and fair education."
2. Write an article for a national newspaper on the topic: "The Irish political system has little appeal for young people."
3. Write an article for a national newspaper on the subject of fee-paying schools.
4. Write a humorous article for a Sunday newspaper on the subject of technology in schools.

TEXT 2

This is an article that focuses on something the world would be better off without. This contribution to the RTE Radio 1 series The Quiet Quarter *was submitted by John O'Keeffe, then Dean of the Law School at Dublin Business School.*

FOR THE RECORD

John O'Keeffe

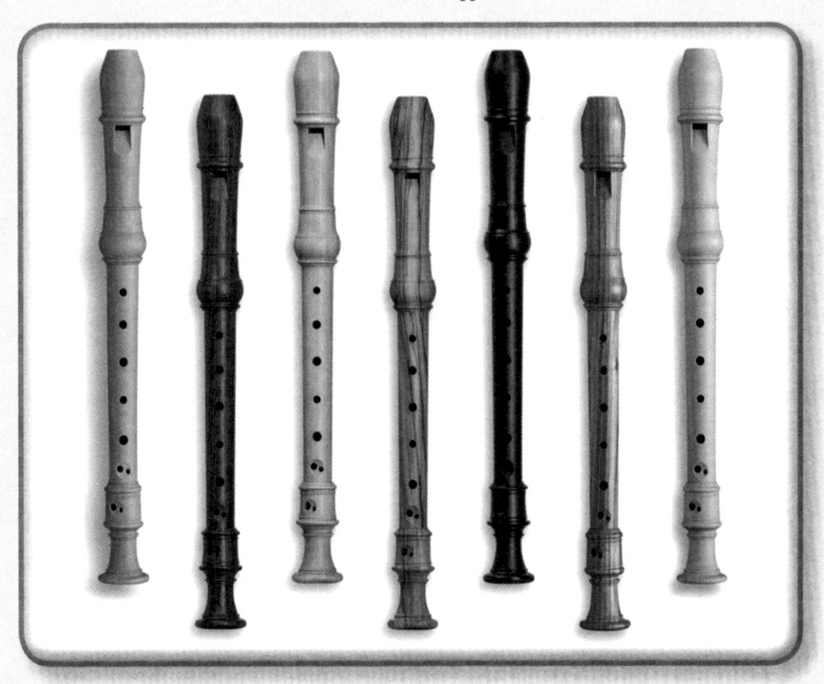

It is a truism that there is no greater hurt in life than to be unloved. This being so, in the world of musical instruments, the recorder must surely play the role of the most wounded of sisters. For those of you who thought that children's loathing of the recorder was simply youthful moaning, you might now wish to reconsider. What we all secretly knew, but were too scared to admit, has now been revealed. Children hate learning the recorder more than visits to Auntie May on a Sunday or family holidays in the mobile home in Courtown.

Research published in Britain has revealed that, in fact, recorders put children off music for life. Apparently, the repetition of "Old MacDonald Had a Farm", on the bourgeois version of a tin whistle, does little to endear the little ones to this musical equivalent of hara-kiri. Not a wonderful legacy for an instrument of torture meant to encourage our love of music from an early age.

If we were all honest with ourselves, we would have to admit that that unusual brown thing which was shoved into our faces as single-digit children looked and sounded awful. The sound was almost secondary to the look. What self-respecting thirteen-year old boy would hang around the school gates hoping to see Mary from Loreto with a packet of Kola cubes in one hand and a recorder in the other? Not many I knew. And why were they always brown? When fashion experts announce that brown is this year's black, they should always include a caveat for recorders.

And there's another thing – I never seem to remember any of us having cases for our less-than-lovely batons. You could, therefore, never hide it – there it was like a plastic Toblerone sticking out of your schoolbag saying to the world, "Look at him – he hasn't a note in his head and so he plays me twice a week with 200 other ingrates!" The sound of recorders is also worthy of mention. No matter how much you practised, no matter how much you listened to Ms Reilly, you always sounded like a wood pigeon with dysentery. Musically, this could discourage some children for life.

One of the remarks that leaps out from the Economic and Social Research Council's paper is: "Children do not associate playing the recorder with their musical role models in the adult world." *Quelle Surprise*, I hear you roar, but this statement does not go to the heart of the problem.

There is no book entitled *Great Recordists of our Time.* Neither James Galway nor Robbie Williams have ever cited the recorder as one of their formative musical influences. Even my own music teacher, whom I met recently after many years, advised me that she dreaded our Friday recorder sessions more than childbirth. High praise indeed for an instrument whose only real value lay in attacking siblings from behind after two hours of beating out incomprehensible interpretations of "Frere Jacques" and "The Wheels on the Bus" – a sort of friendly fire of the musical world.

The truth about the recorder was, and is, that schools continue to encourage its use because it is hard wearing – as I found out when practising with it on my brother's head – and inexpensive. Here's a thought – although I have heard some fine music played on a paper and comb and even a dustbin lid over the years, it does not necessarily follow that durable and cheap means musically useful or melodious.

I know that there will be some of you who feel that the recorder should be made compulsory for the Leaving Certificate and have oral and aural components – that it should be awarded extra points and given the Freedom of Fingal. I beg to differ.

A full state funeral should be offered perhaps, where recorders from around the world might play their last respects. This would then be followed by a simple but moving ceremony in the Phoenix Park when all recorders on the island would be cremated. Then, and only then, can we finally park this terrible part of our history and move on to a brighter, braver new world, where all musical instruments will be loved and cherished. All that is, except one.

NOTES

MY RESPONSE TO THE ARTICLE:	
CLARITY OF PURPOSE:	
COHERENCE OF DELIVERY:	
LANGUAGE OF EXPRESSION:	
HOW WILL THESE HELP ME TO IMPROVE MY OWN WRITING:	
MARK OUT OF 100:	

EXERCISES

Write an article on ONE of the following topics:

1. Write a humorous article for a national newspaper on the one item that you consider the world would be better off without.
2. Write a serious article on the damage science has done our planet.
3. Write a humorous article for your school magazine on the subject of school rules.

TEXT 3

This article by Alex Owens (a Fifth-Year student) was originally penned for Voice, *a school magazine written by pupils for pupils. The language and subject matter appeal to a mature audience of his peers.*

DIARY OF A N00B

My heart pounds as I run haphazardly across the courtyard to the wall of what looks like an abandoned bunker. I crouch low, gravel crunching beneath my weight. Raising the lens to my eye, I survey my surroundings – rusted oil barrels, empty freight containers and endless mounds of sand – but no enemies in sight. Returning the gun to my side, I edge ever closer to the corner, a single bead of sweat running down the side of my face. *So close*, I tell myself, gripping the controller in a death lock as I tiptoe forward. *I just need to*...AARRGH! Splotches of red obstruct my view as gunshots sear the air and pierce my armour, forcing me mercilessly to the ground as I jab at every button, trigger and stick within reach, but to no avail. "KILLED!" blares the screen for the 23rd time today. "Respawn?" it taunts, replaying my pathetic slaughter in the background. Grudgingly, I punch 'A'. Welcome to my (gaming) world.

For as long as I can remember, I've been terrible at video games. *PS 1, 2, 3, PSP, XBox, XBox 360,* Wii, I've played them all, and I've *always* been useless at them. It doesn't really matter what game we're playing either, my ineptitude translates regardless of whether I'm an paratrooper fighting insurgents, Mike Tyson pummeling an opponent or Crash Bandicoot spinning around and dodging crocodiles.

And in the age where stereotypical teenage boys are addicted to "pawning n00bs", "kill ratios" and virtual warmongering in general, my 'problem' has been accentuated; I am the virtual "fat kid" who nobody wants on their football team; I'm picked last, if invited to game at all, and am, without fail, a disappointing teammate and pitiful opponent. I am the ultimate definition of a n00b – the gaming underclass, looked upon with distain (but importantly not pity) by the élite of the gaming world. I've had friends 'kill' me and then ask, "*Who was that? Oh, it was only Alex*".

Every time I think I might have the upper hand, I seem to get bludgeoned, stabbed, punched or zapped before I can say 'bazooka'. In my desperation, I have flouted every unwritten rule of the gaming community.

'Screenwatching', for example, is a major gaming *faux pas*; it involves looking at your opponents' quarter of the screen in an attempt to figure out where they are relative to you.

Unfortunately for me, the supposed advantage that experienced gamers enjoy from this inside knowledge goes over my head and I invariably get mowed down in the few seconds I stop running to take a good look.

Another gaming no-no is staying in one place, waiting for enemies to come to you. Again, cheating doesn't help my chances, as even when a target does come my way, they manage to aim and shoot with devastating precision while I'm fumbling with the ammunition.

Of course, as a serial n00b, I'm quick to support theories that state that gaming culture is bad for society and should be banned, and we should all go back to playing cards, marbles and chasing (all pursuits in which I reigned supreme back in the glorious Junior Infants days). I agree with those who think that shooting games teach kids how to shoot better, boxing games tell them it's good to fight and car games encourage (you guessed it) reckless driving.

I take a cynical view, too, of the supposed 'benefits' of gaming. One friend, for example, claimed that people who play games will make better surgeons because their hand-eye coordination is enhanced. Another suggested that playing war games develops strategic thinking and gives an understanding of military tactics.

I would seriously doubt that my kill:death ratio on *Call of Duty* could have an impact on my ability to take out your appendix, or that my ability as a soldier containing insurgent threats on *COD* would help me to be a better American soldier containing insurgent threats in the real world.

But who is right? Are the social scientists who prescribe a ban simply wounded n00bs like me, sick of rejection and embarrassment and yearning to resurrect the pastimes they were actually good at? Or is there an actual threat here? If someone practises aiming a gun at someone's head five hours a week, are they more likely to replicate it in real life? Or do we trust ourselves to detach our virtual and real worlds?

If we do trust ourselves to stick to the real world, is the problem that we are less sensitive to casualties and war on a larger scale because we experience it daily in our living rooms? Do we take human life for granted when we take pride in finding better and better ways of ending (virtual) life?

All of these concerns must be balanced with the reality that most of the people who play these games are able to very easily distinguish between the virtual and the real (as well as, indeed, right from wrong). I am not worried about my friends becoming lunatics because they play *Call of Duty*. What I am concerned about is how games are developing; how the user experience is more and more first-person; you are holding the gun, shooting directly at opponents. Surely the experience becomes more intense and the lines are further blurred between the real and the virtual words. Surely our gamers will find that line harder to distinguish as the development continues.

But then, maybe they'll be able to tell real from virtual regardless of how intense the gaming experience. Maybe those who can play the game understand it better than those of us who wait on the sideline, hoping we won't get shot. And maybe I'll be better when I can actually hold the gun – in fact, that's it, it's the controller's fault. Roll on *X Box Live Shooter*!

NOTES

MY RESPONSE TO THE ARTICLE:	
CLARITY OF PURPOSE:	
COHERENCE OF DELIVERY:	
LANGUAGE OF EXPRESSION:	
HOW WILL THESE HELP ME TO IMPROVE MY OWN WRITING:	
MARK OUT OF 100:	

EXERCISES

Write an article on ONE of the following topics:

1. Write an article (serious or humorous) for your school publication on the topic: "My experience of games at school."
2. Write an article for your school publication on the topic of teenagers and culture.
3. Write an article (serious or humorous) for your school magazine on the importance of being different.
4. Write an article for a national newspaper on the impact technology has had, and has, on the lives of teenagers.
5. Write a humorous article on why September is the best/worst month in the year.

TEXT 4

This article is by a Fifth-Year student, Rob McCarthy. It was written for a school magazine.

TÍR GAN TEANGA...

National identity is something we Irish hold quite dearly. If you mention the Irish language to certain members of the Irish populace, their veins begin to course with fierce green nationalistic blood (ninety percent of which is usually whiskey). For some, it is essential, it is Ireland and the thought that there are people out there who look upon the language with derision, practically makes them want to explode in a 1916-esque flurry of patriotism. The problem is the balance in the argument whether we should still encourage the language has started to tip towards the deriders in recent years. These forward thinking twenty-first century Irishmen and women are far too busy captaining industry, and maximising whatever it is they are employed to maximise, to waste time resurrecting good old Gaelige.

The problem with Irish is that it is festering in society as an annoyance; it is stagnant culture from another time that has lost its relevance for a large chunk of the population. The purpose of a language is communication. That is what language is ultimately for, nothing else. Some could argue that Irish has failed as a language. Nobody speaks Irish exclusively and those who do speak it frequently also speak English because it's a language that actually works. It is no longer necessary for communication and therefore it is dying, or as they say in Connemara, "therefore it is dying" (because everyone can speak English there).

The very nature of any existence is simply just to exist, to be. Irish is just about hanging on, but that is only because we are forcing it.

The Irish language is no longer natural. It no longer rolls off our tongue. We've replaced the harsh rhythmic utterances of the Irish language with garbled swear words injected sporadically into the English language. Irish is now English with more swearing and better grammar than the variation the British use.

The means by which the language is taught doesn't work either. Unfortunately, yet unsurprisingly really, an analysis of Cathal Ó Searchaigh's poems doesn't make us want to run out into the world and share it with humanity (especially the members of humanity that live in Nepal). A language is supposed to be lived and loved, not analysed. Certainly, modern languages shouldn't be taught this way. If Irish was on par with Latin, then 'studying' the language would work, but it isn't. If we are convinced that Irish is still just about alive, then it should be taught like French or Spanish, whereby it is promoted as something that should be experienced not documented.

The way in which Irish is imparted to the youth is a topic of discussion in its own right but that isn't necessarily a criticism of the language itself. People will still argue that it is essential to our national identity. However, that argument has been countered by some, suggesting that it lends about as much to our national identity as leprechauns and alcoholism, in so far as it doesn't define us as a nation. They say modern Ireland is different. This is where the anti-Irish argument falls flat. What does summarise Ireland if Irish does not? Modern Ireland is effectively defined by its own greed and short-sightedness. Modern Ireland is a culturally indifferent mess. When Ireland finally obtained a bit of wealth in the Celtic Tiger era, it wasn't the real Ireland and it wasn't real wealth. Modest suburban houses costing millions of euro? That's nonsensical, it's a farce and that is not what Ireland is about. The Irish language survived far longer than our 'wealth' did. Irish is something that we created that isn't terrible (unlike most of our disastrous creations).

The interesting thing about Irish is that it's actually quite a nice language. It has a sort of musical element to it, it swings and swoons much like the Irish soul itself. Irish suits us and, though the pinstripe wearing, SUV driving detractors of the language won't admit it, Irish is embedded deep within us. Without it, we are no different to England. This is usually the argument-winning point. Play the "English cards" right at the end and no Irishman will disagree. The thought that we are in any way similar to the old land-stealing, culture-crushing enemy turns us all into nationalists.

Borders and divisions don't make a country (and neither does hatred of other countries). The people and culture are what defines a land. We may have let the Irish language slip, but we shouldn't let it disappear. If attitudes and techniques were changed, there is absolutely no reason why Irish couldn't have a renaissance.

These are just some thoughts on a page, actions are completely different. But it is nice being able to write about this topic "as Bearla" as opposed to in an essay "as Gaelige" that I've been forced to do. That's the key point: something needs to be done to encourage people to want to learn Irish. Ramming it down the throats of helpless students has brought the language nowhere. You never know, if the right steps are taken, in several years I might be writing articles like this in Irish by choice. And best of all, someone might actually read and understand what I'm saying.

NOTES

MY RESPONSE TO THE ARTICLE:	
CLARITY OF PURPOSE:	
COHERENCE OF DELIVERY:	
LANGUAGE OF EXPRESSION:	
HOW WILL THESE HELP ME TO IMPROVE MY OWN WRITING:	
MARK OUT OF 100:	

EXERCISES

Write an article on ONE of the following topics:

1. Write an article for publication in a school magazine responding to the above article.
2. Write an article on the aspects of life that make you proud to live in Ireland.

SUGGESTIONS FOR CREATIVITY

It is important to display some originality and creativity in your written work. There are endless approaches you might wish to try to achieve this. The following pages contain some examples of articles constructed in an interesting and engaging manner.

1. The A–Z format

This is effective if you want to approach a topic in a light-hearted manner. It is also good for expressing opinion and conveying information.

The following extract is from an informative article on fashion for a young people's magazine. The A–Z format makes it look like a glitzy, more lively article.

Example 1

This summer do you want to be stylish and popular? Or are you content to be a social loser? The following article could transform a Roy Cropper into a Thierry Henry or a Cinderella into a Britney Spears.

A is for being **ANONYMOUS**.
A definite no-no when it comes to being stylish. To avoid this, wear Armani. The most unstylish garment ever invented is the anorak, a favourite of train-spotters, bachelors and (some) teachers.

B is for **BLAZERS**. Worn by sailing-club members and ex-public-school boys. They make one look ridiculous. Leaving Cert students (male or female) who take their debating seriously can get away with wearing a well-cut blazer.

C is for **CLOTHES**, obviously. Contrary to what is generally believed, clothes are worn not just for decency or to keep us warm. They are for making us noticed, attractive and for giving confidence. In our increasingly shallow society, first impressions do count. So make sure your clothes say something positive about you.

D is for **DRESSING DOWN**. This is strictly for rebels, losers and socialists/anarchists. What no self-respecting socialite should ever do. Poets and artists can get away with this.

F is for **FCUK**. Yes we got the joke, about ten years ago. This label is way past its sell-by date and is now ever so vulgar. If French Connection U.K. wants you to advertise, you should be paid by them. Too much writing on clothes is not advised.

G is for **GUCCI** bags, shoes and sunglasses, which can fast track you into the world of *Sex and the City*. Your wardrobe can never have too many accessories.

H is for **HAIRY** chests. Men who parade them are so 70s and should be avoided. Obvious exception is on the beach, where Adonis is allowed show his animal physique.

I is for **ITALY** the home of fashion and style. If you want to really impress this summer, then sip cappuccinos, greet friends with kisses and ciaos, and wear the best Milanese fashion.

J is for **JOHN ROCHA**, Ireland's best known designer. His understated style is for the discerning follower of fashion.

K is for **KLEIN**, as in Calvin.

L is for **LYCRA** and leggings, which are largely synonymous. The figure hugging material has been a godsend for mums.

M is for **MEN**. For most of human history, men's fashion rarely moved on from animal skins. Then suddenly at the end of the 20th century, men discovered a whole world of cosmetics and clothes. Most men still need the advice of wives/girlfriends, big sister and even mammy.

N is for **NUNS**. Their fashion decisions are largely made for them. There are also plainclothes nuns who wear normal clothes, but are spotted at a distance of hundreds of kilometres. Old habits die hard!

O is for **OMG**. A once fashionable phrase that is now a sign of being very yesterday.

P is for **POLITICALLY CORRECT**. This philosophy has infiltrated the world of politics and fashion. It is un-PC to wear real fur, clothes made in sweat shops, and anything that granny buys for you. Seriously though, it has made consumers more conscious about the origin of the clothes that are bought. PC is good but preachy.

Q is for **QUORM**. A food fad that lasted for a zillionth of a second in 2006. No one even remembers what it was.

R is for **RADIANT**. All girls desire to look so on a night out.

T is for **TOP**Shop. What a wondrous emporium it is. Men have their equivalent (Topman) and unless you are a goth or a tracksuit wearer, you will know it is the best place to shop.

U is for **UNDERWEAR**. And moving quickly on…

V is for **VEGETARIANISM**. This is a worthy way to live but most veggies don't really bother with something as superficial as fashion. They tend to want to save the planet, and hug trees and visit India. Maybe their time has not come yet and they are prophets of the future.

W is for "**WHEN** will you grow up?" The question often asked of teenagers by parents who are tired of shelving out money on the newest clothes. The answer is never – a fashion sense continues to the coffin.

X usually with an **L** for **ENORMOUS** clothes.

Y is for **YELLOW**. A colour best avoided.

Z is for **ZZZ** – How I feel after composing this article.

It is true that beauty is in the eye of the beholder, and that world of fashion is subjective. But it is also true that bad clothes provoke ridicule and social exclusion while attractive clothes are, well, attractive. Unfortunately, humans are shallow and judge by appearance.

NOTES

WHAT ARE THE STRENGTHS AND WEAKNESSES OF THIS ARTICLE?	
DO YOU FIND IT ORIGINAL?	
WHAT LESSON CAN YOU LEARN FROM THIS THAT MIGHT HELP WITH YOUR WRITING?	

Note the content, tone and expression. **Remember** to frame the **A–Z** within clearly written, purposeful paragraphs.

2. The Open Letter

The 'open letter' can be an effective way of structuring a persuasive article. Although the letter is addressed to one person (or a group of people), it is for general consumption.

Here are some examples of people you could address it to:

- Dear Michael D.,
- Dear Bono,
- Dear Parents of Irish children,
- Dear God,

Before writing, consider your purpose and the tone that you wish to adopt.

Example 2

FEEL THE RAIN

To the moaners who never stop going on about the weather and to the deluded who cannot accept that this island is wet.

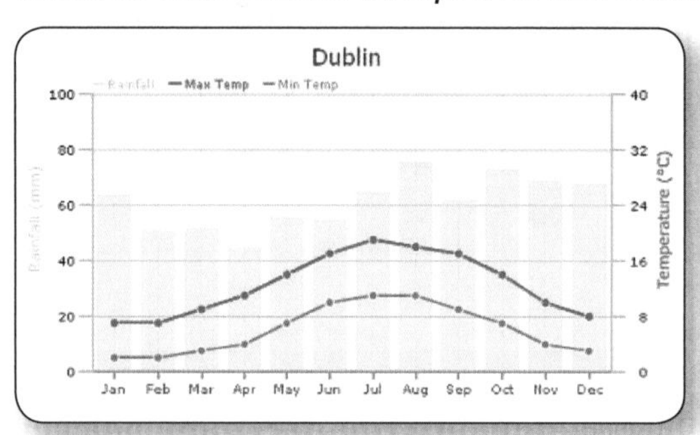

Get over it! Like all addicts you must first accept that you have got a problem. We live on a rock in the Atlantic, further north (in latitude) than Canadian Inuits. We have one of the wettest and coolest climates in Europe. Our mean average temperature in JULY is 15 Celsius. We can expect up to 250 wet days a year. Meteorologically we are depressed, but that is no reason why we should be down in the dumps about the weather. While global warming might have sounded promising to us, it has in fact led to even wetter summers here. We need to get real and to overcome our expectations. Google the Irish climate and you get: "Mild, moist and changeable...abundant rainfall."

Unfounded hope leads to perpetual disappointment, our national characteristic. Did it all start with our early ancestors? Think of the amazing construction that Neolithic man built at Newgrange. Using the sophistication of a stone axe and incredible knowledge of the winter solstice, these early people built a tomb designed to trap the precious rays of sunrise every winter solstice. The labour that went into this must have felt wasted as year after year cloud cover prevented the spectacular show that only happens intermittingly. Did they go home dissatisfied (like we go today when yet another picnic has been ruined?) or did they make a human sacrifice to appease their disgruntlement (like we today might wish to make a pyre of the RTE weather team when another summer ends in unused barbecues and loungers rusting and rotting on sodden lawns)?

There is a disconnect between what we want our weather to be and what it is. This has led to a confusion of who we want to be and who we actually are. We are not Italian, or Australian or American. Not for us planning barbies and family outings to the beach or camping in the great outdoors. We must stop pretending that sunglasses, T-shirts, shorts are needed here where it rains every second day. This just leads to disappointment. Our pale pink skins cannot cope in sweltering heat. When we do get a few hot days we moan about a heat wave that makes us uncomfortable. Let us make do with fake tan (if we must, and it is a safer alternative to sun beds) and sun holidays (we invented the cheap flight, thanks Ryanair!). When we are here on this island, let's have no more pretence. Let us all invest in rainproof clothes and enjoy what we have in abundance: uncrowded beaches; unpolluted rivers and lakes; unpopulated hills. Ireland is a paradise for surfers, canoeists, walkers, horseriders, anglers, golfers, cyclists, and all those brave enough for the outdoors. Forget pretending that this summer is going to be barbecue heaven – it probably will be a washout like most summers are. Our German friends have a saying: There is no such thing as bad weather, only unsuitable clothing. Maybe we should listen to them sometimes.

Moaning about the weather does not make it better. When Evelyn Cusack and Jean Byrne tell us to expect unsettled weather, don't pin your hopes on a trip to the seaside; scattered showers means rain. I would like a bit more honesty. Why do they insist on calling the constant summer rain pattern unsettled? It is completely settled – wet. Get out into it and feel alive!

We are addicted to the weather because when we wake up we still hope for a blue sky even though the weather chart we saw the previous evening had more spirals than decorate the tomb at Newgrange (did our ancestors somehow know about isobars?). If hope doesn't lead to disappointment, it can lead to delusion. How many times do you see people on a bright, but otherwise freezing, day going out dressed like Californian beach bums? Long queues form at the seaside ice-cream trucks, the outside tables are crammed with lunchers, and the loungers are hauled out of sheds. But in an instant a big black cloud has everyone running. Pleasure turns to pain all too quickly. Our forty

shades of green now has a worthy alternative in the fifty shades of grey! Each one a summer's day!

And so to the moaners – who go on endlessly about the terrible weather and the deluded ones who don't acknowledge how truly bad the weather is – I say just cop on. Accept that we live in the clouds (literally – we know this because when a plane approaches Dublin airport it drops down through ten miles of the stuff before landing). Be glad that we can go for comfortable summer walks that are impossible in Spain, Turkey, and Italy. Celebrate what the water gives us (not just great stuff to drink) but to fish in and surf on.

It's the first of June and I am off to Penneys to stock up on raingear, then I will take to the hills and waterways of Ireland to enjoy what this country has to offer. If you want to stay indoors with your faces (de) pressed against windows as if you are in a giant carwash, then good luck. As the folks used to say, a drop of rain never killed anyone.

NOTES

WHAT ARE THE STRENGTHS AND WEAKNESSES OF THIS ARTICLE?	
DO YOU FIND IT ORIGINAL?	
WHAT LESSON CAN YOU LEARN FROM THIS THAT MIGHT HELP WITH YOUR WRITING?	

EXERCISES

1. Write an open letter in which you respond to the text above.
2. Write an open letter in which you address a topical issue of importance to you.

3. The Parody

A parody is where you imitate another work or form, usually for the purposes of ridicule or humour. The best parody has a serious purpose behind it. Is it clear to the reader what is being ridiculed in each of the examples below? Is the style of writing effective?

Example 3

Here are two examples that could be developed further or simply used to illustrate a point.

In a land far away, there lived a silly king who lived in a big white castle. This king, whose name was George, had the biggest and best equipped army in all the world. The people in this land loved their king and his kingdom. Every year on the fourth day of the hottest month, the people celebrated their own greatness.

But in a land of deserts and camels there lurked an evil genius, Ben the Lad. The Lad was a very cunning man. He sent his soldiers dressed as humble travellers to the land of George, killing thousands of innocent people.

Now George was angry. He knew the Lad lived in the desert lands. So he gathered his army and sent them to the desert land. Some people said he should make sure that Ben was there. But he did not listen. So his army attacked the wrong country. Ben the Lad continued to send his evil men dressed up as travellers to George's kingdom. And George continued to attack all the places that Ben never was in...

Or

At this time in a small kingdom, there lived a very clever people. Long used to hardships due to living in a land of rain, they decided the most important thing for them was to build castles. A craze swept the nation. Everybody wanted a castle of their own, some wanted even more than one. The leaders of the country made gold available to help people with this madness. Soon there was not enough gold to pay for any more castles to be built so the leader, Bert, went to the great Kingdom of E to ask for more.

The kingdom of E saw what an industrious people the Oirish were, so he lent more gold than is imaginable. The castle building continued until one day the chief collector of taxes, who had been asleep, woke up and realised there was no money in the kingdom to pay for the nurses and teachers and guards.

The kings of E came and saw the foolishness of the castle-building and asked for all their gold back but there was no gold in the land, only castles that no one could afford to live in...

NOTES

WHAT ARE THE STRENGTHS AND WEAKNESSES OF THESE ARTICLES?	
DO YOU FIND THEM ORIGINAL?	
WHAT LESSON CAN YOU LEARN FROM THESE THAT MIGHT HELP WITH YOUR WRITING?	

EXERCISES

1. Write a creative parody in which you satirise a well-known person or address a problem in society.
2. Write a parody of one of the following. Your article should have a serious intention.
   - Harry Potter
   - Lord of the Rings
   - Twilight
   - A Shakespearean play
   - A Fairy Tale
   - A Hollywood film

10

THE DESCRIPTIVE ESSAY

With descriptive writing, the focus is on creating a sense of place or atmosphere. Although there can be a narrative element, **a descriptive composition does not have to tell a story**.

Topics for descriptive writing can include descriptions of:

- **Events**
- **People**
- **Places**

Good descriptive writing will:

- Create a strong sense of atmosphere.
- Use imagery.
- Vary vocabulary and sentence structure.
- Have an awareness of the sound of the writing.
- Refer to the five senses.

TEXT 1

In this first example, the writer Joseph O'Connor gives a descriptive account of an event. The scene that he describes probably took no more than a few minutes, but the descriptive detail draws it out, so that we feel that we have experienced what happened.

BORDERLINES

By Joseph O'Connor

Prepared for the unexpected

It was about five in the morning and I was somewhere around the border when it happened. I had been in Donegal doing a reading, and I had had to leave very early the next morning to get back to Dublin. I crossed north to look for a garage that was open, and then I headed south. I was driving quite fast along the motorway. If I tell you the truth, I was breaking the speed limit. But I wasn't too worried, because at five in the morning there's no traffic at all. It was quiet and still and in the distance I could see the sun beginning to come

up over the fields to my left, and on my right the vast hulk of Ben Bulben. Van Morrison was on the radio, and I was smoking a cigarette. I was enjoying myself. I didn't know what was going to happen.

suspense sustained

I turned a bend in the road. The scene was like something out of a beautiful dream. There were cherry blossom trees at the edge of the fields all along the motorway, and the breeze was shaking the boughs and showering the road with white petals. It was an extraordinary sight, the white petals raining down on the motorway like so much confetti. And then it happened.

effective short sentence

description

When I recall the whole thing now, I think I first saw the bird when I was about a hundred yards away from it. There were other birds around, whirling around above the motorway, but I think I did actually see this one just sitting still in the middle of the road. I kept going. I got closer and closer to this bird and then suddenly I was a few feet away from it.

detail

It rose up from the ground and spread its wings wide. But then I think either a gust of wind caught it, or it got trapped in the airstream around the moving car, and for one awful moment it hung in the air as though suspended by some invisible filament before it hit the windscreen with a dull and sickening thud that I don't think I will ever forget.

effective onomatopoeia

The whole windscreen went red. It was as though someone had poured blood all over the glass. I jammed my foot down on the brake and the car swerved across the motorway and into the oncoming lane. I felt the adrenalin surging through my limbs and body like a drug. I got out of the car. I could feel my breath coming hard and I could feel my hands and legs shaking. The poor bird was lying on the bonnet of the car, croaking in agony. There was a trail of blood and black feathers all over the metal. The bird flapped its wing and thrashed its head and slipped off the front of the car and fell onto the ground. It was in terrible distress. I found myself talking to it. I actually found myself apologising to the bird for hitting it. It suddenly dawned on me that I would have to kill it.

I am a townie. In my whole life, I have never killed anything larger than a spider. It's not that I am a big animal lover: it just never happened. How do you kill a bird? What was the most humane way of doing it? I looked at the bird, trembling on the road, and then I decided I just couldn't do it. I decided to leave it there. I went to get back into the car, but just as I did so it let out another terrified croak. I knew then that I would have to end its agony.

effective use of questions

I stared at it. Should I try to break its neck or something? Should I just put my hands on its bloodied throat and twist the life out of it? I squatted beside it and went to touch it, but I just couldn't bring myself to do that. I felt ashamed of my own cowardice. I got back up and walked up the road for a while, trying to find a heavy flat stone which I drop on the bird. Maybe that would kill it. Finally I found one. I staggered back down towards the car with the rock in my hands. But by the time I got back to the car I was glad to find that

the bird was dead. I lifted its broken body and threw it by the side of the road.

NOTES

WHAT ARE THE STRENGTHS AND WEAKNESSES OF THIS ARTICLE?	
DO YOU FIND IT ORIGINAL?	
WHAT LESSON CAN YOU LEARN FROM THIS THAT MIGHT HELP WITH YOUR WRITING?	

EXERCISES

1. How does the descriptive writing in this passage add to the power of the piece?
2. How will reading this passage help to improve your writing?
3. Write a descriptive essay on a time when you felt lonely or fearful.

TEXT 2

The author of the following piece, Vona Groarke, is a poet and a teacher of creative writing at Manchester University. This descriptive piece was broadcast as part of the RTE radio series Sunday Miscellany.

THE WAKING CITY

By Vona Groarke

For whatever reason, you just can't sleep. It's four a.m., you have a flight at nine, tomorrow that will wear you out and you should sleep. You try, you really try, and once or twice, you feel it creep up on you, but it's like a shadow and something carried over from the evening before insists it isn't time yet for darkness and lost hours. Outside your window, lamplight stains the footpath and your windowsill and your hand, when you hold back the hotel blind to watch the street for even some small evidence of another life. This city, you see, goes on without you, filling in its night-time hours behind closed doors and curtained windows: nothing is on show, not up the street that only a few small hours ago, you tottered up on too-high heels, all set for the evening ahead. Not down the street, towards the arch and the river, where something, at least, is moving along, allowing itself to change.

You pull on clothes. Faint light is just coming into its own. You think again of a newborn calf unpacking itself from folded legs, trying to find its feet. Like origami in reverse. It isn't even cold. You head first for the docks: if anywhere won't have quite given up on the night before, it will be here. The engines of the navy ships are grumbling away about the years and years it's been since they had anything like fun. No one's on deck. A retinue of yachts and fishing boats trade gossip by the wall. Their names flutter like charms on a bracelet: *Shangri-La*, the *Derring-Do*, the *Milicent*, *Lán Grá*.

You pass a pub with no shutters and no lights. You're looking in the window at the chrome of upturned chairs glinting in a mirror that occupies the full breadth of one wall, and then, when you look harder, at four sets of eyes fixed on you from the corner of the bar: the staff making a night of it, the work done, the place cleared and nobody ready yet to call it a day. You move on.

There's a huge pile of scrap metal at the end of the pier. Rusty fragments of cars and gates and cylinders and pipes and sheet metal and something that looks like a turnip mangle with the words 'Pierce & Son' just legible, poke out of a mass of burnished copper, that in this light, could almost be a midden haul of newly unearthed antiquities: golden torcs and filigree silver and an ambered reliquary with flecks of soil still clinging.

Down by the arch, the river holds sway. You walk the path alongside, flanked on the right by new apartments with all their curtains pulled tight and no light within. You notice a derelict warehouse you never saw before. You're counting its windows when the brakes of the bin lorry at the end of the path pull you up short and you have to start over. "D'ya see those churches, that one and the big cathedral, well they got the whole thing wrong, you know, the whole bloody thing just back to front," he says behind you. The binman has a theory that is something to do with Sundays being Saturdays and the Sabbath being observed on the wrong day. He quotes chapter and verse and doesn't look like he'll draw breath anytime soon. "Good man," you say, "you've obviously looked into it anyway", and before he can register the interruption, you take off. You don't own the morning any more.

A couple swings out of Cross Street singing a song together in a language you don't recognise. They stop ahead of you in front of the record shop and call up a name to the open window above the sign. A blond head pokes out and then a key is thrown that clatters on the road and has the two of them scrambling to beat each other to be the one to pick it up. The woman wins and dangles it in front of the man's face while he tries to get it off her. They don't notice you. You walk on.

Back towards the hotel, a man is wedging open the door of his corner shop. He nods at you and you nod back. A man in a security uniform comes out behind him with a two-litre bottle of Coke and a bouquet of chocolate bars. He nods at you too and, just like that, the morning is suddenly more about the day ahead than it is about last night. You walk into the foyer: the night porter is washing floor tiles. He looks up to tell you the forecast is beautiful.

NOTES

WHAT ARE THE STRENGTHS AND WEAKNESSES OF THIS ARTICLE?	
DO YOU FIND IT ORIGINAL?	
WHAT LESSON CAN YOU LEARN FROM THIS THAT MIGHT HELP WITH YOUR WRITING?	

EXERCISES

1. The detailed description of early morning in a city brings this extract to life. Underline the most effective techniques used by the author.
2. Write a commentary on the use of description in this passage.
3. Write a description of a time in your life when you found yourself in a strange environment.

This descriptive essay was written by a Fifth-Year student, Neasa Owens. She was asked to write a descriptive account of an event that was very important in her life.

THE CONCERT

By Neasa Owens

Steel-cold air struck my face as I emerged from my mum's over-heated car. The Point stood illuminated across the road, a beacon, a Mecca attracting diverse hordes. The dark waters of the Liffey flowed by, a chilly wind ruffling its oily surface. Above, a clear night exposed a sky packed with stars that sent shimmering light from worlds unimaginable.

"Enjoy the concert, love."

"Thanks, mum, I'll text when it's over."

The car snaked away into the fumes of barely moving traffic. Feeling liberated, I crossed the road, ready for a heart-pounding appointment with the stars I was about to see, hear and experience for real.

Queues usually drain me. Tonight, each shoe length drew me closer to the source of my joy and inspiration. I went through imagined set lists of the songs I hoped would be performed. I imagined what would open the show and hypothesised about the choice of encore.

Tickets checked, I wandered through the vaulted entrance. I imagined that this is how early Christians must have felt as they arrived in Jerusalem after a long pilgrimage. Instead of relics, the souvenir sellers peddled T-shirts, posters, albums (some signed), and keyrings, each with my heroes' faces on it. A full hour to go. A smell of burgers, chips, pizzas and hotdogs assailed my nostrils. I was starving and sick all at once. A cold bubbling Coke is what I settled for. Strawing up the drink, I was amazed by the diversity of the punters. From ten to eighty, skinny to elephantine, people on crutches, some with hair, others bald as footballs, some in cool shades, others wearing prescription glasses, a few over-dressed and many under-dressed; this band drew them all. I felt a connection. As if at last I belonged to some secret group that I had never met, but here they were and I was one of them: so many people that in everyday life go about their anonymous lives, but this night had drawn together.

An escalator took me, ascending upwards to my seat. Heaven-bound. Sitting in the semi-darkness, feeling a painful tingle from too much waiting, I began to have doubts. What if the live show was a disappointment? What if the sound was poor? What...

The auditorium dipped into darkness. A voice announced the band. Lights illuminated the stage in a kaleidoscope of crazy colours. Simultaneously, the crowd exploded in an atomic roar. An earth-pounding drum roll was followed by a maniacal guitar solo and the crowd was suddenly a screaming, many-headed, dancing creature. The lead singer came to the microphone and screamed out to all: "Hello Dublin!"

Two hours later, I was waiting beside the dark and murky waters of the Liffey. My mum's car pulled up. I opened the door. "So how was it? Had a great night, did you?"

What could I say? I had been to the stars and beyond. I ascended to pearly gates and met the gods. That tonight was the best night ever? Words just didn't work.

"Yeah. It was good." With that, I climbed into the front seat and stared out at a city that was dull and grey. My mind was on the stars.

NOTES

WHAT ARE THE STRENGTHS AND WEAKNESSES OF THIS ARTICLE?	
DO YOU FIND IT ORIGINAL?	
WHAT LESSON CAN YOU LEARN FROM THIS THAT MIGHT HELP WITH YOUR WRITING?	

EXERCISES

1. Write a descriptive account of opening a present.
2. Write a description of a fireworks display.
3. Write your own descriptive account of a visit to a public event.

TEXT 4

The following composition was written by Sixth-Year student, Jack Murphy. The assignment given was to write a descriptive essay on a sad or joyful family occasion.

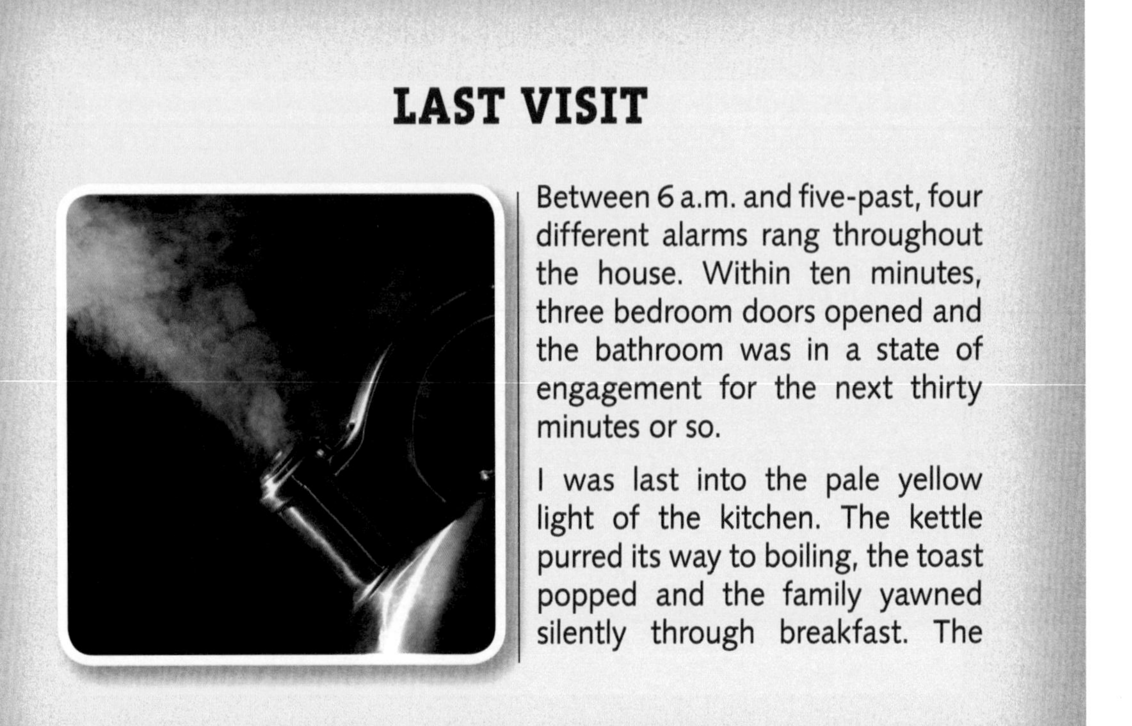

LAST VISIT

Between 6 a.m. and five-past, four different alarms rang throughout the house. Within ten minutes, three bedroom doors opened and the bathroom was in a state of engagement for the next thirty minutes or so.

I was last into the pale yellow light of the kitchen. The kettle purred its way to boiling, the toast popped and the family yawned silently through breakfast. The early morning routine is usually more boisterous, with narky demands and shouts of "I'm first in the shower!" On this earlier-than-usual-morning, there was an unspoken determination to get through the day with the least hassle. My mom's face was grey with tiredness and puffy with tears shed and kept back. My dad was not shielding himself behind a newspaper and I was not moaning about the terrible cereals we have in this house. The kitchen noises this morning were of plates, spoons, water and the odd slurping of tea or crunching of toast.

Within forty-five minutes, the kitchen was quiet; the stillness then spread throughout the house as we all made our way to the car. Even with the dreadful news, mum had organised what everyone would need. A couple of cases were loaded in the boot. Outside, frost covered the ground in a deathlike veil. It was going to be a long drive to the country. Mum got the call that grandmother had died at 10 o'clock the previous night. My uncle was making the arrangements and we would all stay with him for a few days.

The drive through the suburbs was like going through a town in a foreign city, when you arrive on a late night/early morning flight and a taxi takes you through sleeping places you don't know.

As light cracked open the sky, the city gave way to countryside. After a quick pit stop for petrol, coffee and bathroom, the atmosphere in the car changed. Dad broke the ice, recalling other happier trips down this road. There was the time we went to collect Charlie. On the way up to Dublin, he crept into my hood and slept all the way. Charlie was our first pet: a black cat with a smudge of white on its chin. From the time I was five, he was like an appendage to me for twelve years. He had been attacked by an urban fox last year and the family had all wept when we brought him to the vet for the last time. Then there was the time we went down for Gran's eightieth. Her seventy-five living relatives were there. Sons, daughters, grandchildren, a brother, nieces and nephews all converged from the four corners of the globe. The names and faces we had heard about but had never seen made it an amazing celebration. There was the famous occasion that Dad tried a short cut because of roadworks on the main road. That short cut cost us four hours. When we arrived, Gran had gone to bed thinking we wouldn't be coming. When she heard noises outside, she called the police. The local Gardai ended up coming in for a cup of tea but stayed for hours. It turns out Mum knew their family and, in fact, had gone to her first dance with the guard's dad.

Now, the miles disappeared as the stories gave us a landscape of memories to distract us. For the next hour, we all had a "remember when" story and soon were turning up the familiar

country lane with the rusty iron gate that I had to lift and push open. Green paint cracked across the door like some ancient script; the house was cold. In the past, there was always a welcoming blaze of turf, but now a heap of dead ashes lay in the hearth. Mum wanted to stop here before going to the hospital where Gran had died. Houses take on the spirit and life of their owners. But this house was dead. In the kitchen, the blue and white patterned cups and plates stood forlornly on the dresser; this time there was no tea offered. The place resembled a museum. It was a place where time had stopped. We, or at least I, felt like intruders. I thought of the full tide, a sea brimming with life and action and energy and then it falls to a desert of sand. The cottage felt like a desolate beach when the tide is out.

"I suppose we better be getting to the hospital now."

I was glad.

The next few days sped by like a family video. I recall moments such as the sickly warm heat of the church; the kind faces of the locals who wanted to offer their condolences. The moment I had been dreading in the mortuary was not as bad as I had imagined. Granny's skin was yellow and her hair a whitewashed grey, but there was nothing frightening about her. The wrinkles had softened as she lay sleeping eternally.

After four days, it was now time to go. When we pulled up at the cottage for Mum to say a final goodbye to her childhood home, I stayed in the car. I knew that there was nothing more for me to see. Usually, we took something back to Dublin after these country visits: an apple tart, some new spuds, a bag of turf or a 20 note that Gran stuffed in my pockets when my parents weren't looking. When Mum came out, she was holding something.

"I think we better bring Mr Trix with us."

It was Gran's little cat that she had told us all about in her last letter. My uncle didn't need another cat on the farm. I took him on my lap and promised Gran I would look after him for her.

NOTES

WHAT ARE THE STRENGTHS AND WEAKNESSES OF THIS ARTICLE?	
DO YOU FIND IT ORIGINAL?	
WHAT LESSON CAN YOU LEARN FROM THIS THAT MIGHT HELP WITH YOUR WRITING?	

EXERCISES

1. Write a descriptive account of your earliest memory.
2. Write a descriptive account of a memorable journey.
3. Write your own descriptive account of a happy or sad occasion in your life.

TEXT 5

The following is an extract from Bill Bryson's travel book The Lost Continent. *Here, Bryson describes a visit to the Grand Canyon in the United States.*

WHAT A SIGHT

By Bill Bryson

The Grand Canyon was the one vivid experience from my childhood that I could hope to recapture, and I had been looking forward to it for many days. By the time I reached the entrance to Grand Canyon National Park, and paid the $5 admission, snow was dropping heavily again, thick white flakes so big that their undersides carried shadows.

The road through the park followed the southern lip of the canyon for thirty miles. Two or three times, I stopped in lay-bys and went to the edge to peer hopefully into the silent murk, knowing that the canyon was out there, just beyond my nose, but I couldn't see anything. The fog was everywhere – threaded among the trees, adrift on the roadsides, rising steamily off the pavement. It was so thick I could kick holes in it. Glumly I drove on to the Grand Canyon Village, where there was a visitor's centre and a rustic hotel and a scattering of administrative buildings. There were lots of tour buses and recreational vehicles in the parking lots and people hanging around in entranceways or picking their way through the slushy snow, going from one building to another.
I went and had an overpriced cup of coffee in the hotel cafeteria and felt damp and dispirited. I had really been looking forward to the Grand Canyon. I sat by the window and bleakly watched the snow pile up.

Afterwards, I trudged towards the visitor's centre, perhaps 200 yards away, but before I got there I came across a snow-splattered sign announcing a look-out point half a mile away along a trail through the woods and impulsively I went down it, mostly just to get some air. The path was slippery and took a long time to traverse, but on the way the snow stopped falling and the air felt clean and refreshing. Eventually I came to a platform of rocks, marking the edge of the canyon. There was no fence to keep you back from the edge, so I shuffled cautiously over and looked down, but could see nothing but grey soup. A middle-aged couple came along and as we stood chatting about what a dispiriting experience this was, a miraculous thing happened. The fog parted. It just silently drew back, like a set of theatre curtains being opened, and suddenly we saw that we were at the edge of a sheer, giddying drop of at least a thousand feet. "Jesus!" we said and jumped back, and all along the canyon edge you could hear people saying "Jesus!", like a message being passed down a long line. And then for many moments all was silence, except for the tiny fretful shiftings of the snow, because out there in front of us was the most awesome, most silencing sight that exists on earth.

The scale of the Grand Canyon is almost beyond comprehension. It is ten miles across, a mile deep, 180 miles long. You could set the Empire State Building down in it and still be thousands of feet above it. Indeed you could set the whole of Manhattan down inside it and you would still be so high above it that buses would be like ants and people would be invisible, and not a sound would reach you. The thing that gets you – that gets everyone – is the silence. The Grand Canyon just swallows sound. The sense of space and emptiness is overwhelming, Nothing happened out there. Down below you on the canyon floor, far, far away, is the thing that carved it: the Colorado River. It is 300 feet wide, but from the canyon's lip it looks thin and insignificant. It looks like an old shoelace. Everything is dwarfed by this mighty hole.

And then, just as swiftly, just as silently as the fog had parted, it closed again and the Grand Canyon was a secret once more. I had seen it for no more than twenty or thirty seconds, but at least I had seen it. Feeling semi-satisfied, I turned around and walked back towards the car, content now to move on.

NOTES

WHAT ARE THE STRENGTHS AND WEAKNESSES OF THIS ARTICLE?	
DO YOU FIND IT ORIGINAL?	
WHAT LESSON CAN YOU LEARN FROM THIS THAT MIGHT HELP WITH YOUR WRITING?	

EXERCISES

1. "Bill Bryson is a master of the travelogue." Having read the above account of his trip to the Grand Canyon, comment on Bill Bryson's style of writing. Support your answer using references to the article.
2. Write a descriptive composition on a place that is special to you.
3. Write a descriptive composition on a trip that you made to a place of great natural beauty.

Composing a Short Story

INTRODUCTION

A short story is a piece of fiction that is tightly contained in a few pages. Like all good stories, it should have a beginning, middle and end. To work, a short story must be controlled and coherent. Unlike a novel, the space to develop characters and scenes is limited.

What makes a good short story?	**What ruins a story?**
Originality	Predictability
Interesting characters	Stereotypical characters
Exciting plot	Dull plot
Vivid descriptions	Inconsistencies/no description
Accurate dialogue	Poor dialogue
Correct spelling and punctuation	Incorrect spelling and punctuation

When writing a short story, **do not attempt too much**. For example, a story involving intergalactic warfare is very ambitious and difficult to deal with in the short-story format.

The story must not be predictable. Predictable topics include "serial killers on the rampage", "sub scores last-minute goal", and so on.

Short stories open a window into a world – as we read, our imaginations bring this world to life. Writers make their imaginary world real through description, character development and plot.

Stories should begin with an **idea**. You must then create **characters** and a **plot** to carry the idea. Above all, the story must be shaped. Stories can be plot driven or character driven or a mixture of both. All stories follow the shape of an arc.

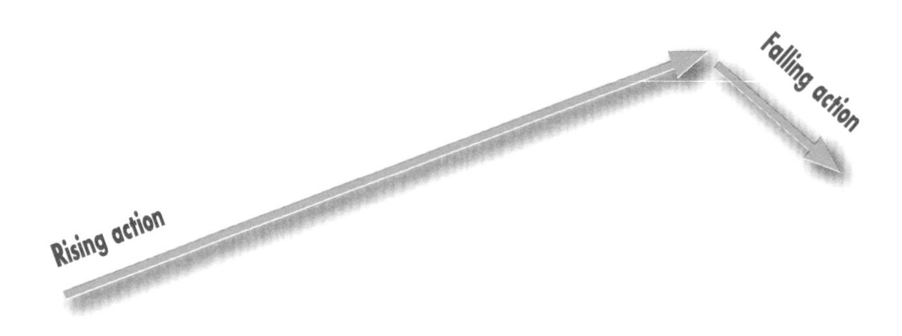

Practice is essential in the writing of a good short story. You will not be able to construct an acceptable story on the day of the examination if you have not practised.

ON EXAM DAY

How long should a short story be? In the exam, you have 90 minutes to plan, structure and write your story. Consequently, your story should not exceed 1,000 words. Roughly 30 minutes should be spent planning character and plot. Do not **force** a story you have already written to fit the titles given if they are not suitable. Of course, something you have written can be **adapted** for the task in hand, but it must work for the question asked.

Under no circumstances should you reproduce a story by somebody else that you have read previously.

The American writer Ernest Hemingway once wrote a powerful story using only six words.

For sale:
Baby shoes, never used.

The impact that this 'story' has on readers is remarkable. Why? It forces us to create a story based on the little, but shocking, information that has been supplied. Our imaginations and emotions respond to the situation.

Leaving Certificate students should aim for 800 to 900 words. This provides adequate space to develop a storyline and character. You should practise writing short stories that concentrate on the formation of plot and/or character.

The *Irish Times* once ran a competition asking readers to submit stories of no more than 500 words.

The following story was submitted by Gaius Coffey and it is an excellent example of what can be achieved in a short space by effective and creative expression.

ALONE, NOT LONELY

By *Gaius Coffey*

You are alone. Of course you are; how else would you have found time to read? It's the difference between alone and lonely. You would not read, could not read, if you were lonely. Every scene would be encased in glass so that you could see but not participate.

You are not lonely. You are gloriously alone with your thoughts. Comfortable thoughts about the pleasing warmth of your mug, disappointed thoughts that you've eaten the last of your chocolate and confusing thoughts about a story you saw on the news. It would be dizzying if a friend tried to lead your thoughts along so many directions, but even the thoughts you don't enjoy are comforting because these are your thoughts and you are alone.

You know the noises you hear in the kitchen are just the creaks of the oven cooling and the cold draft on your neck is just the way the living-room door doesn't quite seal and the sensation of being watched is nothing more than a relaxed mind amusing itself.

You are relaxed, even your eyelids are drooping and the thin paperback in your hands is about to fall. With the gentle distraction of the noise of an open fire, you think about crumpets and jam. You wish you had had the foresight to buy some this afternoon when you were shopping. You remember carrying the heavy bags through to the kitchen and placing your keys – no, you don't remember placing your keys anywhere.

You don't remember placing your keys anywhere because you left them in the door and you know it is too late to fetch them as a hand clamps over your mouth and jerks your head backwards. You feel a knife against your throat and have never felt lonelier, now that you are not alone.

EXERCISES

1. How does the writer create a feeling of suspense? What is unusual about the telling of the story (consider the use of the second-person for the narrative voice)?
2. Consider the last sentence and comment on its effect.
3. Write a short story that has a dramatic ending.

BUILDING A CHARACTER

The laziest approach is to use 'I' as a main character. Only do this if you are willing to flesh out this character. You must help your reader to imagine the main character. First-person narratives often fail because the main character is thinly drawn. To succeed, a first-person narrative must be driven by a strong voice.

Before beginning to write any story, you must know your main character. Use rough work to build the character's profile, e.g. age, gender, job, physical characteristics, taste in clothes, etc. What gives this character individuality? What distinguishes this character? Think of famous characters such as Sherlock Holmes, Homer Simpson, Harry Potter, Macbeth, Hamlet, Romeo, *Twilight's* Edward and Bella, Holden Caulfield, and so on. Each of these is very easy to imagine. What makes each so memorable? Is it a physical detail, or the clothes they wear, or an aspect of their personality?

Sometimes, it is a good idea to picture the character's house and environment. What is in it? What CD has been last played? Who last called him/her by phone or mobile? What book/newspaper has been read by the character? Who is closest to him/her? Is there a photograph in the room?

Verisimilitude is the term for making your writing as real as possible.

Have a clear view of the character before beginning to write. It would be useful to decide the following attributes in advance:

- Age
- Name
- Physical details
- Clothes
- Personality
- Job or school/college

The advantage of having carefully constructed characters is that you can then imagine different scenarios for them. When you write your story, one or two well-chosen details will convey what your character is like. It is better to suggest what a character is like, rather than bluntly tell the reader what a character is like.

WORKING ON PLOT

A plot is the ordered sequence of events. The structure of a story is much tighter than in an anecdote.

Consider the following aspects of plot:

- Series of events
- Structure
- Flashback
- One or two characters
- Creation of tension and suspense
- Unpredictable twist
- Conclusion: climax and resolution

A story should begin **just before** something interesting/life-changing is going to happen to the main character.

The story should be manageable in the space you have to tell it, so avoid being too ambitious.

Imagine that you as a storyteller can peer into the life of a character just before something important is going to happen. Remember that you have limited space to describe the character, the setting and the action as it unfolds.

If you are a visual person, plan using little **storyboards** – these are often used in **film-making** and help with **plot** construction

Here is the plot outline of a sample story

EXPOSITION	Description of city – create atmosphere. Helen sitting in a taxi regrets calling Frank a 'loser'. Little details – "mascara stained cheeks."
DEVELOPMENT	Flashback to an hour before. Romantic evening together in restaurant. Sipping coffee and jointly spooning a tiramisu. Argument begins when she asks if the job-hunting has gone well. He leaves.
COMPLICATION	Back in taxi, Helen realises she had always liked his happy-go-lucky nature. Recalls how the relationship began. Romantic story that began in Greece. He was backpacking; she was staying in luxury hotels. Opposites attract.
CLIMAX	Asks taxi to go back to restaurant. He is gone. She goes to his place to make up. But he has decided she is right. They are too different.
RESOLUTION	One year later: Helen's bank has downsized and she was let go. Frank has had an offer for his novel in which he charted their romance.

Most of the above story is set in a taxi as Helen thinks over her relationship. We should be pulled into the action. A good writer will be able to reveal the inner world of the main character.
If you took this idea, would you paint Helen in a sympathetic light? Would you focus on her learning a lesson? Or would you concentrate on her misfortune?

Before deciding, you should build a profile of the two main characters. As your imagination gets to work, you might want to change details. Which of the two characters do you sympathise most with? What city would you set it in? How would you handle the flashback sequences? Would you try to write some paragraphs from Frank's perspective?

TELLING A STORY

The success of a story lies in the **way it is told**. Your job as a writer is to bring the characters to life, to create atmosphere, to make the story seem real. Recognise that you are composing a story.

Once you have an interesting idea, a structured plot and believable characters, you now have to write. The way you tell a story is as important as the story itself. It must have its own rhythm, so that it reads in a flowing manner. Characters and action must also be consistent.

SHOW, DON'T TELL!

Before reading some examples of stories, it might be useful think about **how** to write.

There is no shortage of stories to tell. There are many events that have happened to us that can be the raw materials of a short story. We also have hundreds of stories that we have read or seen as films that can be adapted to make interesting stories of our own. Originality comes in the telling of the story. Working on character and plot takes effort, but you will be rewarded.

For example, assume that you have been asked to write an imaginative retelling of *Little Red Riding Hood* for a modern readership. One could dress the main character in the prevailing fashion of today/the forest could be a shopping centre/the wolf a junkie. Using your imagination, you can transform this into a relevant and interesting story.

CREATIVE WRITING

Use descriptive adjectives. Write in colour. Refer to the senses.
Vary your verbs and choose the most powerful and expressive ones.

Avoid the use of weak adjectives, such as:

- He saw **this** girl.
- There were **a lot** of people there
- She was **nice**.

Instead, you could write:

- He glimpsed an angel in Uggs and a fawn jacket.
- The room buzzed with chatter and fun.
- She was reserved, yet mysterious.

Be specific in your descriptions. Look at the following sentences:

- He was driving a big, new car.
- She was dressed to the nines.

These could be re-written as:

- He surveyed the cul de sac from behind the windscreen of his 4-litre Mercedes.
- In her cream Armani suit, her Gucci leather-banded, gold-buckled shoes and her chic Valentino shades, Vicki made an impression.

The extra detail gives vitality to the description, but be careful not to overdo it.

Contrast these sentences:

Tim **went** to school.	Tim **crawled** to school.
Julie **saw** her father in the distance.	Julie **glimpsed** her father in the distance.
Jeremy **talked** all evening.	Jeremy **nattered** on all evening.
Cliona **got up** at seven.	Cliona **dragged** herself from her bed at seven.

EXERCISES

Insert the most effective verbs in the blank spaces below.

Sunlight (__________) on the water all afternoon. Julie (__________) under the umbrella, every so often she (__________) from her book to see what the others were doing. Her father (__________) in the heat, oblivious to the sun. Willing to suffer that night for his indulgence, her mother had a stack of magazines which she (__________) all day. Her two brothers (__________) all afternoon in the sun, (__________)ing, (__________)ing, (__________)ing.

He lifted his head and (__________) the air. There was a smell he couldn't quite (__________).
Noise (__________) from the kitchen. He (__________) to the door. Inside people were (__________)ing, (__________)ing and (__________)ing. He wanted to (__________).
He (__________) someone (__________) his name. His heart (__________) in his chest. They had (__________) his birthday.

We are so used to films and television giving us pictures that we can be lazy and expect a reader to see what we see in our imaginations. In writing a story, you must be an artist: paint the scene; use the senses to create an atmosphere.

Use the Senses

In creating a scene, it is a good idea to include references to the senses. **Remember** that an atmosphere can be created by referring to **touch**, **taste**, **sight**, **smell** and **sound**. Read the following passage and note how the senses are used to create a certain atmosphere.

After break, the class reeked of newly peeled oranges, crisps, sugary drinks and sweat. But worse were the energetic squeals and high-pitched screams of the First Years. The yellowing walls and green floor tiles were sickening. In front of him were twenty of the most hardened boys in the area. Half had threatening bleached hair. Most of the others had an array of gels and grease in theirs. A few were completely shaved. The sweat of his hands made his briefcase seem heavier and more cumbersome than ever. He could feel a little bead of sweat making its way down his back. The acidic tang of canteen coffee clung to his tongue. The May sunlight exploded against the window. The class settled. But Mr Kingston remained silent, merely standing there, wondering if it was all a waste of time.

EXERCISES

1. What do you learn about Mr Kingston from the descriptive details?
2. What words would you have used to describe the sunlight on the window?

Create Atmosphere

Read the following passages, paying particular attention to the way in which the atmosphere is created, and then answer the questions that follow.

TEXT 1

She dropped the petals of the red rose one by one into the river. The surging waters took them all away. One little petal drifted to the quietness of the shallows. It was hemmed in by stones. But it wanted to escape. It persisted, finally dislodging itself, and in a flurry chased after its fellow petals. The tears which had been flowing down Lee's face all evening were now gone. She was absorbed by the sense of purpose of that frail petal. It was not giving up. The other petals were clear of all obstacles. So what if it took this one a little longer. This little solitary petal was determined. Soon the red smudge was gone from sight. But she could picture it charging ever onwards. That is what she knew she must do. Giving up was not an option.

EXERCISES

1. What do we learn about the character in this paragraph?
2. What is her mood and how is this conveyed?

TEXT 2

We tried Monopoly for forty minutes. But every minute one of us would look at the splattered window and curse. Day-time television chatter covered the patter of rain but our attention was not on Oprah/MTV/reruns of Friends/Sky News as we channel-hopped for an hour. The Game Boy was broken, and last night's DVD was hardly worth another look. We mucked about in the kitchen and were hunted out by mum with her "I'm sick of cleaning up after you" rant. 18 July. Middle of summer. Nothing to do, nowhere to go. The excitement of June was long gone and it was too early to feel the nervous expectations of beginning again in September. Boredom.

EXERCISES

1. Is this an effective depiction of boredom? Give reasons for your answer.
2. Pick out the words/phrases that best convey the writer's feelings.
3. Write an evocative paragraph to describe one of the following:
    - An emigrant's first job.
    - A teenager's first date.

- A person working as Santa Claus in a department store.
- A young person leaving home for the first time.
- A grandmother/grandfather at an important family celebration.
- A person winning a prize.
- The scene at a pop concert.

Choose words with care!

WRITING DIALOGUE

If you are using direct speech, you must **make it sound natural**.

Getting the rhythm of everyday speech is a skill. Listen to phrases that you hear every day. A character from Dublin should not sound like one from an American movie.

Expressions and Dialect

As well as being accurately punctuated, dialogue should sound real. It should try to reflect the way that people actually speak. Expressions can vary according to region, county or country. When next watching a soap opera, for example, examine the language and note the colloquial expressions.

However, be careful and **do not use clichéd speech or outdated phrases**, such as the following, which will be unconvincing for the reader:

- "Begorrah, top of the mornin' to ya, yer honour!"
- "I say, that's a spiffin' top hat you have there, my good man."

Read the following. What do we learn from these sentences?

- The faucet is broken and we have no diapers.
- Isn't it frightfully hot today?
- The lift is broken, mate, you'll have to use the apples and pears.
- I cannae remember the wee lad.
- It's, like, just so not cool to go on holiday with your parents.

In writing direct speech, it is acceptable to use colloquial expression, but avoid vulgar and inappropriate language. A good writer can achieve much by not upsetting or offending the reader. If there is dialogue, make sure that it is punctuated properly.

DIALOGUE

- Give a new line for each speaker.
- All direct speech should go inside quotation marks.
- Punctuation marks go inside quotation marks.
- Use capital letters for the names of people and places.

EXAMPLES

1. The group stood on the corner chatting.
"What'll we do now?" Finbar asked.
"Hit the beach," suggested Siobhan.
"I'm sick of the beach," Roy grumbled, pulling a face. "It's full of surfing dudes."
"Don't be so negative. Just because you can't swim, you think the surfers are poseurs," pouted Siobhan.
"Let's just chill here," Derek said, as he tapped a text.
"Better idea," interrupted Carla. "Why don't we get a video? *American Pie 7* is out."
"Whose house?" quizzed Finbar.
"Mine, if you like. As long as no one raids the fridge like last time," Carla implored.
"Let's go then," Roy exclaimed.
With that, they unglued themselves from the fence and headed towards the town.

2. "I'm asking you for the last time, Tony. Where were you on Monday at around midnight?" Detective Willis probed.
"Don't remember," Tony Clarke replied in a smug slow-motion-drawl. "Maybe I was watching the stars, contemplating infinity."
"Don't be smart. We have you on CCTV at 11:39pm, just three minutes walk from the robbery. Anyway, for the record, Monday was raining," insisted Willis.
"Who said anything about the sky? I was looking at pictures of stars in a book at home. With the rain, I'm sure that CCTV footage of yours is kinda useless. Hardly HD, 3D quality, right?" said a cool Clarke, gazing straight back at the increasingly irked detective.
"Let's play it your way then. We'll go to your place. If you have a book with the stars in it, I won't arrest you. If you're lying, we'll take you in for questioning and we will make it tough for you," Willis intoned.
"Hey, that's harassment. Oh yeah, I remember, I went to bed early that night. The stars I saw must have been in me dreams. Angelina and Brad, yeah, I must have dreamt of them, like. And I am sorry if I can't show you me dreams." Clarke now smirked. He knew they wouldn't take him in just yet. He was going to do everything to make the police work on this one.

EXERCISES

1. Read the **two** examples of dialogue above. What makes each one effective?
2. Write out a short passage in which dialogue is used to convey two contrasting characters. In your answer, remember to punctuate according to the proper rules. Provide a new line for each new speaker. Words spoken must go in quotation marks (including the full stop/question mark/exclamation mark).

EXAMPLES OF SHORT STORIES

In the stories that follow, ask yourself these questions as you read through them:

- What do we learn about the main characters? What problem are they faced with? How do they respond to this? Are they changed as a result?
- Trace the plot development. Is there a moment of suspense? Where is the climax of the story? Is the resolution successful?
- What is the main point of the writer's style? What use is made of description/dialogue/imagery?
- How is atmosphere created?
- Is there a theme? Maybe a lesson to be learned?

EXAMPLE 1

Read the following piece written by a student and mark it out of 100. Make sure that you note both the ***positive*** *and* ***negative*** *elements. The student was asked to write a story about the beginning and end of a relationship. This story is by a Fifth-Year student, Lucy Penwell.*

LOSING OUT

I will never forget the look on Gary's father's face when I saw him at the hospital. I knew it was my fault. If only I had not been so selfish, none of this would have happened.

It was Ciara who was really into him at first. She was obsessed with him all through Fifth Year. He was a great soccer player. Centre half and centre of attention – that was Gary. Ciara really wanted to see him play in the final and like the good friend I was I went along. It was a really big deal in school. We had banners and songs, and loads of supporters. The finer points of the game were lost on me, but every time Gary headed the ball, or kicked it forward, Ciara cheered and I leapt and hollered. I think Ciara was a little embarrassed by my antics. When the buses brought us back to school we all took turns to lift the cup. When it was my turn, I realised it was much heavier than it looked. The silverware pulled me back as I held it over my head. I was falling over but suddenly its weight disappeared and I heard a voice: "What about we meet up on Saturday. I promise I won't bring this with me"

I could not believe that I had a date with Gary. I rushed over to tell Ciara. She promised me she was all right about it. But Ciara was not great at hiding her true feelings.

Gary was a romantic. He arrived in a Mercedes, one that his dad was trying to sell in his garage. From the boot, he lifted out a gargantuan box of sweets for Mum and a bouquet of flowers for me. Gary was like a number of different perfect guys all rolled into one. He was quiet but hard-working in class; a magical footballer; a dutiful son; and a real charmer. That first date was perfect. He booked a table for four at a great restaurant and, because he knew that my friend Ciara was without a boyfriend, he had persuaded his best friend Robert to ask her out. Everything was great about that night. I never knew a boy to be so interested in the day-to-day goings-on in the life of his girlfriend. He was the kind who made you feel special.

When my parents went on holidays, Ciara suggested we should have a party at my house. All my friends said let's do it, so I suppose I couldn't let them down. That afternoon we made the house into a red-hot party zone. Some of Gary's football friends were there.

I had made a special CD of the most exciting party tunes I could think of. At the height of the party, I stepped outside for a blast of fresh air. I met some of the smokers from school, and we had a chat about this and that. When I got back I saw Ciara with her arms wrapped around Gary as Bonnie Raitt screamed out "I'm holding out for a hero 'til the end of the night". That was Ciara's favourite song and there she was with Gary. She was pretty wasted. I rushed over to him.

"Gary, I'm starving. Maybe we could get some food. The chipper is still open."

"Of course, babes, I will pop down in a minute."

I knew he was trying to be polite to Ciara, but a blind jealousy choked my reason.

"No. Gary, I am starving, I need food. Now. Why don't you take the keys of Mum's car? The keys are on the back of the kitchen door." I knew he could drive any car. Didn't he spend every Saturday in his dad's garage?

When he went to get his jacket, Ciara came over to me. She knew I was angry with her.

"Why did you send Gary out?" she asked. "Jealous? Anyway, I thought you were off chips. Should he really be driving?"

"Gary never drinks," I said. "Not like some, who can't handle theirs."

I exploded, a barrage of words shot from me. I called her a tramp and said I never wanted to see her again. How dare she come to my party and attempt to take my boyfriend!

I ran up to my room and cried. I knew I was over-reacting. But once the tears started, they rained down my face like when you drive through a carwash. My make-up was ruined. Snivelling, I took out the cosmetic bag and started to paint myself into a presentable shape. I promised myself that I would apologise to Ciara. Everything was going to be OK.

When I got downstairs I couldn't find her. I was told that when I had fled upstairs, Ciara had been very sick, so Gary decided to drop her home on his way to the chipper. That was Gary: so thoughtful, so considerate. The front door bell rang and I rushed to thank Gary and tell him how sorry I was and what a great guy he was.

It wasn't him. Standing in the porch was a garda. My first thought was that the busybody neighbours had called the police to complain about the music. The garda wanted to know where the owner of the red Mazda 131 D 25671 was. I told them mum was on holiday. A few half-heard words were all I could understand: "Crash…two teenagers…hospital…who to notify…"

The yellow light in the hospital waiting room gave everything a deathly glare. At 2am, Gary's dad came into the room. "It's my fault. It's my fault," was all I could blubber. He put his arms around me and cried. He told me that Gary had died ten minutes ago. The girl in the car was in a bad way, but would recover.

I knew that no amount of mascara and lipstick would ever be able to paint over my shame.

NOTES on your response to this story

DID YOU FIND THE CHARACTERS BELIEVABLE?	
WAS THE STORY ENGAGING?	
WHAT ASPECTS DID YOU LIKE / DISLIKE?	
WHAT CAN YOU LEARN ABOUT WRITING A STORY FROM YOUR READING OF THIS ONE?	
AWARD THE STORY MARKS OUT OF 100.	

EXAMPLE 2

Students were asked to write a story in the form of a diary about an important time in their life. Here, John Winston takes an imaginative approach to the task. As you can see, research has been done in order to get the time and setting right.

ME, TOO

Monday, 6/2/78: Mount Temple 0-Belvedere 38. My dad is trying to be supportive but he wore that "I told you not to get your hopes up" look after the game. Mum is inwardly delighted that (a) I survived the rugby season without facial scarring and (b) I can concentrate on the Mocks. School was strangely normal today; everybody except me seemed to expect to lose. Realised that while I was busy playing rugby all season, others were studying. A lot to do. Next door, Mr Flanagan is at his DIY again. Just finished my first English essay in yonks: "Ireland of the future". Can't concentrate, going to watch Brideshead Revisited. Helps me dream of university. Only time the family sit together.

Wednesday, 8/2/78: Worked all evening yesterday and still I have done little more than sort notes. I have really missed the non-rugger friends. Paul stopped by for coffee. He is putting together a band. He wants me to put my talents to use by helping out. That's just what I need - another diversion. Mum thinks he is too cocky. Girls seem to like him though.

Friday, 10/2/78: Got back my essay. Miss G gave it a B, which is a big achievement. But wants to know why I think Ireland is going to be declared bankrupt, offered for sale and bought by the US. Paul got a B+ for a story about the first Irish worldwide rock star. It was good but he has been listening to Bowie for the last year and I don't think Miss got the cheap references. Tonight is his first gig. Gotta go.

Saturday, 11/2: Paul's gig was great. Hardly recognised the lads. I did door, collected thirty quid. Since 8pm, I have studied maths and Irish. Mum wants me to help with shopping this afternoon. Dad is looking in newspapers for a job. Mr Flanagan is continuing to hammer and drill. Haven't seen his missus for a while.

Sunday, 12/2: What is it about work? One full week stuck in the books has convinced me that I know so little. This time last week I was in "blissful ignorance", as my old history teacher might have said. Flanagan's cat (Roxy) has taken up residence in our kitchen. Where is Mrs F? Paul called over to insist that I become his manager. He thinks getting a C in economics shows I have promise. Told him I'd better concentrate on studies. "Your decision, your loss," he said, as he left. Mr Flanagan was bringing in six-foot planks. Kinda coffin-sized.

Thursday, 16/2: Working well. Haven't seen much of Paul, nothing of Mrs F, and little of my family all week. Roxy is now spending as much time at my desk as I am.

Friday, 17/2: Absolutely knackered. My training schedule was less taxing than this studying. At last, I feel I am getting somewhere. Made out two predictions for Leaving Cert results. In one, I was crazily optimistic.

Maths C	Economics A	French B
English B	Irish C	
History A	Physics B	

Then I thought of the worst scenario; what if Yeats doesn't come up, what if I freeze during the orals, what if Mr F does a full house conversion in the first weeks of June. This is my revised prediction:

Maths D	Economics B	Physics D
English E	Irish D	French D

I will either be a law student next year or putting up posters for Paul. Getting back to the books.

Friday, 27/4/78: Feeling ashamed for not writing in a couple of months. But I have been busy.
Mrs F is fine. She was visiting her sister in Leeds and while she was away Mr F built her a new kitchen. That also explains why Roxy preferred kipping here. I am now officially a swot. Only go out once every two weeks. Paul is no longer Paul. He is Bono and his group is U2. He doesn't think the educational system works. Me ma still doesn't trust him. Work. Work. Work.

Monday, 15/8/78: Results out. Uni here I come. Can't believe I did so well. Going to meet the lads tonight. Got a congratulations card from the neighbours. Feeling bad about what I was thinking; must have been all the pressure I was under.

NOTES on your response to this story

DID YOU FIND THE CHARACTERS BELIEVABLE?	
WAS THE STORY ENGAGING?	
WHAT ASPECTS DID YOU LIKE / DISLIKE?	
WHAT CAN YOU LEARN ABOUT WRITING A STORY FROM YOUR READING OF THIS ONE?	
AWARD THE STORY MARKS OUT OF 100.	

EXAMPLE 3

This story was written by a Transition Year student as part of a school short-story competition. It was a winner. The topic that Rory Doyle was given was 'Moving House'.

Another Place

By *Rory M. Doyle*

"That it, then?"
I nodded, and Derek the removal man turned back to the van, gave a wave to his driver and went to the back to lift the ramp, close the hatch and seal up the contents of my previous life.

You don't really want removal men to be efficient and clean; you want them to be burly, and surly, beer-bellied, with pie-breath and greasy hair. You want them to pause, rub their aching backs and take a sharp intake of breath: "Dunno about that, governor, isn't on the agenda."

You want chipped cups, splintered furniture, mashed boxes, lost boxes. Delays. Traffic jams. Running over time. Running out of time. You want stuff stored in the wrong rooms, too-heavy-to-move tea chests dumped in the passage, stuff left behind to be collected, or not, three shame-faced weeks later, after seven increasingly irate phone calls from the new homeowner. You want inefficiency, damage and loss. In fact, if you were in my position, you would want the removal men to simply forget to arrive; you'd want the estate agent to lose the contracts shortly before the exchange takes place; you'd want the utility companies to forget to switch.

And you'd want your wife not to have left you.

Derek snapped shut the padlock on the back of the van, nodded in my direction and walked around to climb into the passenger seat. With a cough of black smoke, the diesel engine fired up and the driver wasted no time in crunching it into gear and thrusting it out amongst the blaring horns of midday Dublin traffic. Some of what was in the back of the van was coming with us to our new home, but a lot more was to be dropped off at the auction house later. The way I felt at that moment, it could have all been taken direct to a landfill.

This is not what I asked for, I told myself, as I slipped the door keys into an envelope, sealed it and pinned the envelope to the wall just inside the front door. Then, after folding my copy of Derek the removal man's manifest and slipping it into my pocket, I took one last look along the hall, past the front room door, past the dining room door, to the kitchen, where we'd eaten every mealtime for years, first as man and wife, and then man and wife and child, and lately, as father and son. On impulse I stepped back inside, walked along the hall to the kitchen door and took one last look inside, imagining us some seven years ago, seeing again the chaos of a young, happily married couple and their baby boy, eating breakfast, getting ready for work, talking, being a family. I saw this picture in my head, felt the sorrow of what I'd never have again, and then, having faced my grief, it faded. Quietly, almost reverentially, I closed the door and, taking a purposeful deep breath, I walked back along and out through the front door, turned and slammed it shut on my old life.

Feeling somehow lighter, I walked down the steps from what had been my front door and across the road to the car, to where Danny was sitting absorbed in his book. I opened the driver's door and got in; "Ready for an adventure?" I asked him, fastening my seat belt, adjusting the wonky rear-view mirror until it seemed prepared to stay in one position long enough for me to be able to ascertain that we weren't going to be crushed by a speeding juggernaut or a fire-engine, and I turned the ignition key.

He nodded, still looking at his book, "Sure", and reached over and patted my head.

"What's that for?" I asked.

He looked up at me, "I'm on your side, Dad. That's all."

"You're eight. You don't get to be on someone's side at eight."

He smiled knowingly and went back to his book.

On the third attempt, the engine of our brand-new, seven-year-old Fiat managed to fire up; I adjusted the mirror again, signalled and pushed out into the traffic. We drove out of the street where I'd lived for nine years, without looking back. Though that could have been because the rear-view mirror had slipped down and sideways once more, giving me a clear view of the passenger side dashboard air-vent.

"I like adventures," Danny said, after about ten minutes.

I rubbed his hair, "So do we all."

"Don't mess up my hair," he told me. "It's got gel on."

"Sorry."

"It's ok."

"When did you start wearing hair gel?"

"Daaad!"

We drove south, across the river, and the traffic was lighter than usual, this still being the school holidays. Danny looked up and asked, "Where are we?"

"Adventure country," I told him.

"Cool."

Fifteen minutes later, we turned into a cul-de-sac that contained a row of large but fairly decayed Victorian houses surrounded on three sides by large equally dilapidated blocks of 1960s neo-Brutalist social housing. Our apartment was in the basement of the house with the removal van parked outside. I pulled between the removal van and a skip, jerked on the handbrake, and turned off the engine. "Come on," I said.

Danny climbed out and went for a look round while I unlocked the door for Derek and his assistant. Then I went and sat on the wall, watching Danny running around.

From this vantage point, I could look up at the back doors and broken windows of the council flats opposite; I could count the satellite dishes and scan the walkways and stairwells where, no doubt, the feral underclass would prowl of an evening, dealing drugs, stealing phones from pregnant fifteen year-olds, and stabbing each other.
Danny was running off some energy, exploring nooks and crannies around the cul-de-sac, and I was letting the removal men do their job, and the sun was setting behind a tower block.

"Don't go too far," I shouted.

He ran over to me, "What?"

"I said, don't go too far."

"OK."

I went to mess his hair but remembered his warning about the hair gel, so instead asked, "Well, what you think?"

He looked around as the glooming evening spread from shadow to shadow; streetlights were flickering on at random, doorways and corners beginning to look threatening. He looked back at me and whispered, "Bandit Country," his eyes glittering, and then he ran off to explore some more.

NOTES on your response to this story

DID YOU FIND THE CHARACTERS BELIEVABLE?	
WAS THE STORY ENGAGING?	
WHAT ASPECTS DID YOU LIKE / DISLIKE?	
WHAT CAN YOU LEARN ABOUT WRITING A STORY FROM YOUR READING OF THIS ONE?	
AWARD THE STORY MARKS OUT OF 100.	

EXAMPLE 4

A Sixth-Year student, Anna Polanski, who has been learning English for six years wrote this story in response to the title 'An Immigrant's Tale'.

AN IMMIGRANT'S TALE

By Anna Polanski

The slow, shuffling feet stepped ever closer to the doorway. Most wore unseasonal runners in all states of disrepair. Then there were the shoes. The men were identifiable by workmen's boots, laced and slip-on leather shoes, some polished, most not. Women were more obvious. Long boots tucked into jeans predominated. Though two pairs of high-heels stood out, especially the lipstick-red ones that were disappearing in the doorway and now the owner could not be seen.

Anna examined her own footwear. These faithful Crocs had served her well. How many miles had she clocked between kitchen counter and tables? Seven years, six days a week, eight hours a day. In that time, she had two serious boyfriends, kept a rabbit in the apartment, went on five trips back home and two holidays to Greece. And learnt English. She remembered reading once when you are drowning that your life flashes before your eyes. Now, as she approached Hatch 4, on this freezing December day her life in Ireland was unfolding before her.

Last evening she got out a pen and paper and tried to make an inventory of her life: 28 years old, entitled to €150 a week, €3,500 saved. To return or not to return? Five friends had already gone back. There will be opportunities there during the Euro 2012, and with her English and experience she could get work. She thought of her mother. Didn't she tell her that Zibby called every few weeks asking for her? At school everyone thought that they would be married before everyone else. Did she still want that? Want him? If only the coffee shop had stayed open, she wouldn't have to make a choice.

At the counter, she handed her documents and had the card stamped.

"Go to post office and get money," the man couldn't even be bothered to speak correct English to her. She tried not to be too offended. Maybe many people with foreign names could make do with such precise instructions.

"Thank you," she replied and headed back out into the chill. On the way to the post office, she passed Marks and Spencer's and remembered the first time she had treated herself to the luxury of one of their prepared dinners. Irma and herself had just moved into the apartment. Anna was celebrating being made assistant manager (€10 an hour). They both set up the new laptop and skyped all those they knew back home. It was that night she decided that the only thing she needed to make it perfect was a pet. On the farm, they had always cats and dogs. She knew the lease had excluded these. A rabbit seemed the ideal solution. Espresso was a perfect name for her. Oh, he was slow but the colour of the froth on top of a creamy espresso was exactly like him.

The post office was next. She remembered all those letters, cards, money orders she had sent home from here. This time she felt different. She had business to do, money to collect. She felt strange getting money in this way. The people here, though, had always been friendly, especially when she was buying postcards.

She handed in her benefit card.

"There you go. Fifty and fifty and fifty is a €150, and ten and ten and ten is thirty, makes thirty cent. One hundred and fifty euro and thirty cent." That was it. For the next week. Anna thought of going to the little coffee shop where Irma used to work before she went back home, but then stopped herself. Two euro could be better spent.

Across the road from the post office, Tommo stood watching. A woman hobbled out, her handbag held in front of her with an old woman's grip. He knew what was in it: €200, bus pass and small change. Probably a lottery card and a lotto slip. Keys definitely. Something religious. He changed his mind. "Bad bleedin' luck, robbin' an oul' one. Unless you really have to." He already had his second target in view. OK, she was young and therefore stronger, but if you give them a fright there's usually no problem. Her bag was less easy to predict: a mobile, defo. Some cash, keys, maybe some bank cards and a credit card, possibly. He followed. Already he was tightening his veins in the expectation of a fix. He now knew the perfect place. Once she gets to the crossing, slam into her, grab the bag and leg it down the side street.

Fifteen minutes later, Anna was at the Garda station reporting the crime.

"Do you remember anything about your attacker, miss?"

"Nothing. Except his shoes. They were Nike. Brand new. Yellow."

"Is that all?" replied the Garda, as he wrote "no description" in his report.

At about the same time, Tommo was ditching Anna's bag, and clutching the one hundred and fifty euro and thirty cent. "Glad it wasn't an Irish one, bleedin' foreign spongers," he thought.

That evening, Anna logged onto www.aerlingus.com for the flights to Warsaw.

NOTES on your response to this story

DID YOU FIND THE CHARACTERS BELIEVABLE?	
WAS THE STORY ENGAGING?	
WHAT ASPECTS DID YOU LIKE / DISLIKE?	
WHAT CAN YOU LEARN ABOUT WRITING A STORY FROM YOUR READING OF THIS ONE?	
AWARD THE STORY MARKS OUT OF 100.	

EXAMPLE 5

The previous texts were written by students. The following story, on the other hand, was written by a master storyteller, James Joyce. You should read it very carefully.

Joyce wrote a collection of short stories called Dubliners *in which the following story appears. Read it and notice how effectively Joyce uses the short story to bring the reader into the world of the main character. Take note of the following aspects:*

- Creation of atmosphere through description.
- The development of the main character's dilemma.
- The unfolding of character.
- The manner in which the story builds towards its climax.

EVELINE

James Joyce

She sat at the window watching the evening invade the avenue. Her head was leaned against the window curtains and in her nostrils was the odour of dusty cretonne. She was tired.

Few people passed. The man out of the last house passed on his way home; she heard his footsteps clacking along the concrete pavement and afterwards crunching on the cinder path before the new red houses. One time there used to be a field there in which they used to play every evening with other people's children. Then a man from Belfast bought the field and built houses in it – not like their little brown houses but bright brick houses with shining roofs. The children of the avenue used to play together in that field – the Devines, the Waters, the Dunns, little Keogh the cripple, she and her brothers and sisters. Ernest, however, never played: he was too grown up. Her father used often to hunt them in out of the field with his blackthorn stick; but usually little Keogh used to keep nix and call out when he saw her father coming. Still they seemed to have been rather happy then. Her father was not so bad then; and besides, her mother was alive. That was a long time ago; she and

her brothers and sisters were all grown up her mother was dead. Tizzie Dunn was dead, too, and the Waters had gone back to England. Everything changes. Now she was going to go away like the others, to leave her home.

Home! She looked round the room, reviewing all its familiar objects which she had dusted once a week for so many years, wondering where on earth all the dust came from. Perhaps she would never see again those familiar objects from which she had never dreamed of being divided. And yet during all those years she had never found out the name of the priest whose yellowing photograph hung on the wall above the broken harmonium beside the coloured print of the promises made to Blessed Margaret Mary Alacoque. He had been a school friend of her father. Whenever he showed the photograph to a visitor her father used to pass it with a casual word: "He is in Melbourne now."

She had consented to go away, to leave her home. Was that wise? She tried to weigh each side of the question. In her home anyway she had shelter and food; she had those whom she had known all her life about her. Of course she had to work hard, both in the house and at business. What would they say of her in the Stores when they found out that she had run away with a fellow? Say she was a fool, perhaps; and her place would be filled up by advertisement. Miss Gavan would be glad. She had always had an edge on her, especially whenever there were people listening.

"Miss Hill, don't you see these ladies are waiting?"

"Look lively, Miss Hill, please."

She would not cry many tears at leaving the Stores.

But in her new home, in a distant unknown country, it would not be like that. Then she would be married – she, Eveline. People would treat her with respect then. She would not be treated as her mother had been. Even now, though she was over nineteen, she sometimes felt herself in danger of her father's violence. She knew it was that that had given her the palpitations. When they were growing up he had never gone for her like he used to go for Harry and Ernest, because she was a girl but latterly he had begun to threaten her and say what he would do to her only for her dead mother's sake. And no she had nobody to protect her. Ernest was dead and Harry, who was in the church decorating business, was nearly always down somewhere in the country. Besides, the invariable squabble for money on Saturday nights had begun to weary her unspeakably. She always gave her entire wages – seven shillings – and Harry always sent up what he could but the trouble was to get any money from her father. He said she used to squander the money, that she had no head, that he wasn't going to give her his hard-earned money to throw about the streets, and much more, for he was usually fairly bad on Saturday night. In the end he would give her the money and ask her had she any intention of buying Sunday's dinner. Then she had to rush out as quickly as she could and do her marketing, holding her black leather purse tightly in her hand as she elbowed her way through the crowds and returning home late under her load of provisions. She had hard work to keep the house together and to see that the two young children who had been left to her charge went to school regularly and got their meals regularly. It was hard work – a hard life – but now that she was about to leave it she did not find it a wholly undesirable life.

She was about to explore another life with Frank. Frank was very kind, manly, open-hearted. She was to go away with him by the night-boat to be his wife and to live with him in Buenos Ayres where he had a home waiting for her. How well she remembered the first time she had seen him; he was lodging in a house on the main road where she used to visit. It seemed a few weeks ago. He was standing at the gate, his peaked cap pushed back on his head and his hair tumbled forward over a face of bronze. Then they had come to know each other. He used to meet her outside the Stores every evening and see her home. He took her to see The Bohemian Girl and she felt elated as she sat in an unaccustomed part of the theatre with him. He was awfully fond of music and sang a little. People knew that they were courting and, when he sang about the lass that loves a sailor, she always felt pleasantly confused. He used to call her Poppens out of fun. First of all it had been an excitement for her to have a fellow and then she had begun to like him. He had tales of distant countries. He had started as a deck boy at a pound a month on a ship of the Allan Line going out to Canada. He told her the names of the ships he had been on and the names of the different services. He had sailed through the Straits of Magellan and he told her stories of the terrible Patagonians. He had fallen on his feet in Buenos Ayres, he said, and had come over to the old country just for a holiday. Of course, her father had found out the affair and had forbidden her to have anything to say to him.

"I know these sailor chaps," he said.

One day he had quarrelled with Frank and after that she had to meet her lover secretly.

The evening deepened in the avenue. The white of two letters in her lap grew indistinct. One was to Harry; the other was to her father. Ernest had been her favourite but she liked Harry too. Her father was becoming old lately, she noticed; he would miss her. Sometimes he could be very nice. Not long before, when she had been laid up for a day, he had read her out a ghost story and made toast for her at the fire. Another day, when their mother was alive, they had all gone for a picnic to the Hill of Howth. She remembered her father putting on her mother's bonnet to make the children laugh.

Her time was running out but she continued to sit by the window, leaning her head against the window curtain, inhaling the odour of dusty cretonne. Down far in the avenue she could hear a street organ playing. She knew the air. Strange that it should come that very night to remind her of the promise to her mother, her promise to keep the home together as long as she could. She remembered the last night of her mother's illness; she was again in the close dark room at the other side of the hall and outside she heard a melancholy air of Italy. The organ-player had been ordered to go away and given sixpence. She remembered her father strutting back into the sickroom saying:

"Damned Italians! coming over here!"

As she mused the pitiful vision of her mother's life laid its spell on the very quick of her being – that life of commonplace sacrifices closing in final craziness. She trembled as she heard again her mother's voice saying constantly with foolish insistence: "Derevaun Seraun! Derevaun Seraun!"

She stood up in a sudden impulse of terror. Escape! She must escape! Frank would save her. He would give her life, perhaps love, too. But she wanted to live. Why should she be unhappy? She had a right to happiness. Frank would take her in his arms, fold her in his arms. He would save her.

She stood among the swaying crowd in the station at the North Wall. He held her hand and she knew that he was speaking to her, saying something about the passage over and over again. The station was full of soldiers with brown baggages. Through the wide doors of the sheds she caught a glimpse of the black mass of the boat, lying in beside the quay wall, with illumined portholes. She answered nothing. She felt her cheek pale and cold and, out of a maze of distress, she prayed to God to direct her, to show her what was her duty. The boat blew a long mournful whistle into the mist. If she went, tomorrow she would be on the sea with Frank, steaming towards Buenos Ayres. Their passage had been booked. Could she still draw back after all he had done for her? Her distress awoke a nausea in her body and she kept moving her lips in silent fervent prayer.

A bell clanged upon her heart. She felt him seize her hand:

"Come!"

All the seas of the world tumbled about her heart. He was drawing her into them: he would drown her. She gripped with both hands at the iron railing.

"Come!"

No! No! No! It was impossible. Her hands clutched the iron in frenzy. Amid the seas she sent a cry of anguish.

"Eveline! Evvy!"

He rushed beyond the barrier and called to her to follow. He was shouted at to go on but he still called to her. She set her white face to him, passive, like a helpless animal. Her eyes gave him no sign of love or farewell or recognition.

NOTES

DID YOU FIND THE CHARACTERS BELIEVABLE?	
WAS THE STORY ENGAGING?	
WHAT ASPECTS DID YOU LIKE / DISLIKE?	
WHAT CAN YOU LEARN ABOUT WRITING A STORY FROM YOUR READING OF THIS ONE?	
AWARD THE STORY MARKS OUT OF 100.	

SECTION 5

SAMPLE PAPERS

EXAM ADVICE

BEFORE EXAMS

Ensure that you have prepared yourself adequately. This will involve plenty of practice with all of the types of question that are asked on the paper. **Practice is crucial to achieving a good mark.**

The earlier chapters of this book addressed the skills that are needed to answer:

- **COMPREHENDING A**
- **COMPREHENDING B**
- **COMPOSING**

During the two years prior to the Leaving Certificate exam, you should have comprehensively studied these chapters.

Knowing what to expect

Past papers give you a good indication of what to expect. Each new exam, however, presents a different challenge. You must be flexible and prepared to adapt what you know to the actual exam paper that has been set.

Acquaint yourself with the Criteria of Assessment that has been provided (see page 111). This will give you an indication of how the examiner will mark your paper.

Use your time fully. **Paper 1 is 2 hours and 50 minutes.** Therefore, you should divide your time in a way that ensures you complete the questions within the allocated time.

There will be a Comprehending section divided into three or four texts. Each text will be followed by Comprehending A and Comprehending B questions. You must answer one Comprehending A and one Comprehending B question. The Comprehending A and Comprehending B answers must relate to different texts – in other words, you cannot answer on the same text for both questions.

- **Comprehending A** (50 marks): expect to spend **45 minutes**.
- **Comprehending B** (50 marks): expect to spend **40 minutes** (you might save 5 minutes here for an extra 5 minutes on the composition).
- **Composing** (100 marks): expect to spend **85 minutes**.

ADVICE: Do not spend time answering two **Comprehending A** questions or two **Comprehending B** questions. Be decisive in making your choice.

DURING THE EXAM

The best way to settle into the exam is by reading the texts and the questions. Give yourself 10 minutes to scan through them, looking at the topics, questions and functional exercises. Also, carefully go through the composition choices: mark the ones that you will consider doing.

When you have decided your texts and Comprehending A, Comprehending B, and (possible) composition, then give yourself over to answering Comprehending A.

COMPREHENDING A

Read the text in the most detailed and focused way that you can. Do not neglect the short introduction. Look closely at the questions, as they will guide your reading.

Next, read the first question. Underline or highlight key word(s) in the question and then reread the text with this question in mind. Highlight and underline the passage for aspects that will help your answer.

- Plan the answer by addressing the key word/words in the question.
- Have three or four main points that you will use to support your argument.
- Support your points with reference/quotation from the extract. Keep quotations short.
- Write a strong conclusion that ties everything together.

Do this for each question and answer. The more practice you have done, the better prepared you will be when the exam comes.

Use the following scheme to structure your answer:

- An introductory paragraph in which you address the question and lay out your argument/ thesis.
- Three/four paragraphs in which you address major points using relevant support.
- A short conclusion.

Remember that good answers are well-focused, well-supported and well-written. Poor answers show insufficient understanding of the extract, do not address the question and are poorly supported.

COMPREHENDING B

The choice you make is very important. There are some functional exercises that you will find easier than others to complete.

- Ensure that you understand the task you have been asked to do.
- Make a plan of what your approach will be. Take into account your audience, content, layout and register.
- Make timing a priority. Unnecessary time spent on a Comprehending B task is time taken from your composition.

Depending on the specific task you have been asked to complete, your answer should be no more than 400 words. That said, you might complete the task in 300 words. The exact length of an answer is not of great consequence as long as you complete it. Long rambling answers, however, are counter-productive. Understand the task, audience and the layout.

COMPOSING

There is a substantial choice in this section of the examination. Make sure you have read each before committing yourself.

You will probably have a preference for a particular type of composition, but ensure that you understand the task you have been asked to do.

Spend at least 20 minutes planning your answer. You are going to write a substantial piece of work that will have to hold the reader's attention.

The work that you have done throughout the previous two years will be of enormous benefit at this stage.

Sample Composition Questions

Understand the task by reading the following questions carefully.

EXERCISE 1

"...17-year-old male protagonist with a darting gaze..."

Write a short story in which the central character is a rebellious teenager (male or female).

The lead-in written in *italics* is not the question. The instruction is in **bold**. Here, the task is to write a story about a rebellious teenager who may be male or female.

EXERCISE 2

"...a living classroom..."

Write an article (serious and/or light-hearted) for a school magazine about your experience of education over the last number of years.

Again, the words in **bold** type contain the instruction. You do not have to refer to "living classroom" in your answer.

EXERCISE 3

"...the dreamtime of my own imaginings."

Write a personal essay on the topic of daydreams.

Once again, the words in **bold** type contain the instruction.

These three compositions are very different in terms of content and how they communicate with the reader. We have different expectations when we read a short story than when we read a magazine article.

A personal essay is not a story written in the first person. It is a reflective piece that may contain an element of narrative but its main purpose is to allow you to reflect upon a topic.

A short story is driven by plot and/or character. It is a creative work that must contain a shape or structure, so that there is movement from an opening situation, through development, complication, climax and resolution. Stories can be first or third person. In either case, character development is important.

A magazine article must communicate with the reader. Everything depends on how successful you are at grabbing attention at the beginning and sustaining this to the end.

REMEMBER

- Take time to read instructions.
- Use a highlighter to underline relevant points during your reading of texts.
- Do not write without purpose.
- Plan your responses to questions.
- Always be sure of the task in answering questions.

Notes

SCHOOL

TEXT 1

These extracts from Ruairi Quinn's autobiography, Straight Left: A Journey in Politics, *describe a series of events from his final year in school.*

A JOURNEY IN POLITICS

By the time I was sixteen, my personal interest in religion, spirituality and belief began to intensify. Influenced initially by Camus but now provoked by writers including Robert Graves, James Joyce, Evelyn Waugh, J.D. Salinger and Ernest Hemingway, I began to question my received set of religious beliefs. At home, my father, a devout Catholic, attended mass every day during lent and we – my brothers – went with him. His commitment had an influence on me despite my growing reservations and in Blackrock I joined the Legion of Mary in 1963…

During [that] sixth year, I was busy painting and had decided to study architecture, which appealed to me because it was both artistically and socially engaged. I came to this decision slowly over two years. While I loved painting, I did not want to become a teacher, which at that time was the only route open to me to continue with art. Alongside my intention to be an architect, I developed my interest in politics. I continued to follow current affairs, but felt that the type of political debate taking place at the national level did not tackle the concerns I considered important. The poverty of distant Africa was brought into our classrooms by our returned missionary teachers. The inequalities at home were to be seen in the row of cottages across from St Vincent's Hospital where a home for six or more people was the size of a single room in my home. Among the books I had read, such as Steinbeck's *Of Mice and Men*, was a clear direction towards the construction of a different political reality…

Towards the end of the first term of sixth year, Stephen Coughlan [school friend] showed me a newspaper report of how the Cambridge Union in Britain had restructured its normal debating configuration to replicate the United Nations. I proposed the idea to the sixth year Debating Society Committee and they agreed. Our UN General Assembly would be all participants and no audience. Twenty countries were selected with a controversial agenda in mind.

We needed an authoritative president, because some people did not think that the set-up would work, and could degenerate into chaos. Father Walter Finn, ex-padre to the Eighth Army during the Second World War, accepted the position.

We had to match the individuals and the states as best we could. The hard men and the tough guys from 6C, were to be representatives from Khrushchev's USSR and Castro's Cuba...

To run onto the pitch at Lansdowne Road as an eighteen year old is a daunting experience. Fired up with the tension in the dressing-room, with its smell of fear and nervousness, combined with the deep odour of wintergreen, we charged out onto the field. Earlier that year I had submitted a scene inspired by rugby as my painting for the Caltex art competition. The main assessor, John Fitzmaurice Mills, was complimentary and told me privately he thought I had caught perfectly the angst of the prisoners, enclosed in their cramped cells. I explained to him that it was a rugby team, togged out in a crowded dressing-room! The pale blue and white horizontal stripes of the Senior Cup team jersey could easily be mistaken for a prisoner's uniform.

In the second half of the match, our scrum-half, Liam Hall, slid over the line from a scrum close to the Terenure line. It was the only try of the match and ensured victory. I don't think I'll ever forget the emotion that these intensely contested games evoked.

EXERCISES

COMPREHENDING A

1. From reading this extract, what is your impression of the young Ruairi Quinn's involvement in school life? Support your answer with reference to the extract.
2. What indications are there that Ruairi Quinn would later get involved in politics? Support your answer.
3. Do you find this an interesting extract? In your answer, make reference to both the content and style of the writing. Support your answer with reference to the extract.

COMPREHENDING B

Write out the text of a speech for radio that you have been asked to deliver on the subject of supporting charities.

TEXT 2

This article is written by Kevin Williams, a lecturer in education, and was published in the Sunday Tribune.

Why students need to sit examinations

Examinations generally suffer from a pretty bad press and in a way this is hardly surprising as human beings do not much like being examined. The criticism of examinations, particularly of the Leaving Certificate, is part of a received orthodoxy which finds fault with much in the educational system. There are some points about the nature of examinations which do not seem to be widely recognised or understood and may therefore be worth saying.

Basically, we need examinations to tell us how we have got on in whatever it is we have been learning, whether this be science, history or a language or learning to swim, to play the piano or to drive a car. And sometimes it is important to find out how we have been doing in respect of a fairly extensive area of knowledge or skill.

For this reason, we often wish to find out about an individual's competence, not so much at the different stages on the way to acquiring a skill, but rather at the end of the process of learning. While continuous assessment has its place, we also need to know what a learner can do at the end of a course.

In some school subjects, we are much more interested in the student's achievement as a result of, rather than while engaged upon, a course of study. In assessing competence at foreign languages, for example, we like to know not simply whether students can conjugate the present tense of regular verbs but whether they can handle a whole range of linguistic tasks.

One advantage of the terminal character of the Leaving Certificate is that it gives an indication of how students can perform over a wide range of tasks at the end of the course of studies.

Sometimes, too, it is important to know how we are doing in relation to other learners. This does not mean that we are intrinsically competitive but rather that in many spheres of learning it is necessary to have an idea of what the *norm* of achievement is within the activities in question.

Human activities also have *criteria* of success built into them. And, in determining the criteria of success at such activities as swimming or mathematics, willingness to try hard and other positive personal qualities, however admirable, are not relevant.

We might, for example, wish to applaud a student's interest in the German language and willingness to do his best to learn it but if the same student fails to acquire even the most elementary mastery of vocabulary or syntax, then we have to say he has been an unsuccessful student of German.

This is not to deny the importance of positive personal qualities and of the school's duty to develop these qualities. But we need to treat with caution claims that personal qualities should be formally assessed.

Not only is it difficult to design credible forms of assessment in the area of personal qualities but it is even more difficult to determine precisely what has been the specific contribution of the school to this aspect of education.

And there is another issue in such assessment, which needs to be considered. If, for example, young people were to be chosen for sought after courses of study on the basis of their personal qualities and social skills, we could find ourselves with competition to be charming, gracious, considerate or thoughtful. This could affect the honesty of the teacher-pupil relationship and lead to a rather bizarre new version of the much maligned 'points system'.

One last point. Learning for examinations is sometimes said to compromise the educational value of an activity. Although it would be foolish to deny that this can happen, it is hardly inevitable.

There is no doubt that human beings tend to act for multiple motives and that there will be some tension inherent in a system which uses academic success for instrumental purposes. But because the outcome of learning is used to determine suitability for further education or for employment, it does not follow that all learning conducted in this context is motivated by crude personal ambition.

There is no reason why students studying for the Leaving Certificate examination should not also derive pleasure and satisfaction from their study. And experience and observation suggest to me that many do.

EXERCISES

COMPREHENDING A

1. According to the writer, why are exams (such as the Leaving Certificate) so important? You must offer support from the text.
2. *"We need to treat with caution claims that personal qualities should be formally assessed."* According to the writer, what are the main problems in assessing personal qualities? You must support your answer.
3. Do you find this to be a convincing argument? Refer in your answer to both the style and content of the article.

COMPREHENDING B

Write a letter to the editor of an Irish national newspaper in which you air your views on an aspect of the educational system that you feel strongly about.

TEXT 3

In the powerful opening chapter from the novel Hard Times, *Charles Dickens presents us with Sir Thomas Gradgrind as he visits his model school. He is talking to the teacher of the school, Mr M'Choakumchild, and a school inspector. The story is set during the industrial revolution and Mr Gradgrind is a well-meaning utilitarian, who held the belief that the greatest good for the greatest number must determine social policy, and that what is good is measurable and quantifiable.*

HARD TIMES

"Now, what I want is, Facts. Teach these boys and girls nothing but Facts. Facts alone are wanted in life. Plant nothing else, and root out everything else. You can only form the minds of reasoning animals upon facts: nothing else will ever be of any service to them. This is the principle upon which I bring up my own children, and this is the principle on which I bring up these children. Stick to facts, sir!"

The scene was a plain, bare, monotonous vault of a schoolroom, and the speaker's square forefinger emphasised his observations by underscoring every sentence with a line on the schoolmaster's sleeve. The emphasis was helped by the speaker's square wall of a forehead, which had his eyebrows for its base, while his eyes found commodious cellarage in two dark caves, overshadowed by the wall. The emphasis was helped by the speaker's mouth, which was wide, thin and hard set. The emphasis was helped by the speaker's voice, which was inflexible, dry and dictatorial. The emphasis was helped by the speaker's hair, which bristled on the skirts of his bald head, a plantation of firs to keep the wind from its shining surface, all covered with knobs, like the crust of a plum pie, as if the head had scarcely warehouse-room for the hard facts stored inside. The speaker's obstinate carriage, square coat, square legs, square shoulders – nay, his very neckcloth, trained to take him by the throat with an unaccommodating grasp, like a stubborn fact, as it was – all helped the emphasis.

"In this life, we want nothing but Facts, sir; nothing but Facts!"

The speaker, and the schoolmaster, and the third grown person present, all backed a little, and swept with their eyes the inclined plane of little vessels then and there arranged in order, ready to have imperial gallons of facts poured into them until they were full to the brim.

EXERCISES

COMPREHENDING A

1. Comment on the use made of descriptive writing in this passage. You must illustrate your answer with reference to at least three features of style.
2. What do you think is the writer's main purpose in his depiction of this school scene? Give reasons for your answer.
3. Compare and contrast the above with your own experience of education. Support your answer with reference to the text.

COMPREHENDING B

Your school principal is interested in setting up a school website for students. He has asked you for suggestions as to what might be on this site that would be useful to students. Write a letter detailing your suggestions.

TEXT 4

Song and Images

Another Brick in the Wall (Lyrics - Part 2)

We don't need no education
We don't need no thought control
No dark sarcasm in the classroom
Teachers leave them kids alone
Hey! Teachers! Leave them kids alone!
All in all it's just another brick in the wall.
All in all you're just another brick in the wall.

We don't need no education
We don't need no thought control
No dark sarcasm in the classroom
Teachers leave them kids alone
Hey! Teachers! Leave them kids alone!
All in all it's just another brick in the wall.
All in all you're just another brick in the wall.

(*Roger Waters*)

EXERCISES

COMPREHENDING A

1. Read the lyrics of the song 'Another Brick in the Wall'. Do you think this song is relevant to today's teenagers? Give reasons for your answer.
2. You have been asked to choose a visual (from the ones displayed above) for a CD cover for the re-release of this song. Which one would you choose? You must give persuasive reasons.
3. Overall, do you think the set of images gives a fair depiction of education? You must refer to all of the images in your answer.

COMPREHENDING B

Your school magazine has organised an interview with the Minister of Education. Submit five questions that you think the minister should be asked and explain why you think these questions are worth asking.

COMPOSING

1. *"Students should derive pleasure and satisfaction from their study."*
   Write a personal essay on your experience of secondary school.
2. *"We need examinations."*
   You have been asked to deliver a speech to the parents of senior students on the topic of 'Preparing for the Leaving Certificate'. Write out the text of the speech you would deliver.
3. Write a humorous article for your school magazine on the joys and tribulations of school shows.
4. A debate is to be held in your school. The motion is "Schools are poor environments for effective learning". Write out the speech you would deliver. You may argue for or against this motion.
5. *"...a plain, bare, monotonous vault of a schoolroom."*
   Write a descriptive account of twenty-four hours in the life of a school building.
6. *"Leave them kids alone."*
   Write an article addressing the depiction of Irish teenagers by the media.
7. Write a story that begins with a student sitting outside the principal's office.
8. *"During Sixth Year, I decided to study architecture."*
   Write a personal essay on your plans for the future.

SPORT

TEXT 1

This is an extract from an essay from the 1940s by the writer George Orwell. In it, the writer addresses the negative aspects of competitive sports.

PLAYING TO WIN

Nearly all sports practised nowadays are competitive. You play to win, and the game has little meaning unless you do your utmost to win. On the village green, where you pick sides and no feeling of patriotism is involved, it is possible to play simply for fun and exercise: but as soon as the question of prestige arises, as soon as you feel that you and some larger

unit will be disgraced if you lose, the most savage combative instincts are aroused. Anyone who has played even in a school football match knows this. At the international level, sport is frankly mimic warfare. But the significant thing is not the behaviour of the players but the attitude of the spectators and, behind the spectators, of the nations who work themselves into furies over these absurd contests, and seriously believe – at any rate for short periods – that running, jumping, kicking a football are tests of national virtue.

As soon as strong feelings of rivalry are aroused, the notion of playing the game according to the rules vanishes. People want to see one side on top and the other side humiliated and they forget that victory gained through cheating or through the intervention of the crowd is meaningless. Even when the spectators don't intervene physically they try to influence the game by cheering their own side and "rattling" opposing players with boos and insults. Serious sport has nothing to do with fair play. It is bound up with hatred, jealousy, boastfulness, disregard of all rules, and sadistic pleasure in witnessing violence: in other words it is war minus the shooting.

Instead of blah-blahing about the clean, healthy rivalry of the football team and the great part played by the Olympic Games in bringing the nations together, it is more useful to inquire how and why this modern cult of sport arose. Most of the games we now play are of ancient origin, but sport does not seem to have been taken very seriously between Roman times and the nineteenth century. Then, chiefly in England and the United States, games were built up into a heavily-financed activity, capable of attracting crowds and rousing savage passions, and the infection spread from country to country. It is the most violently combative sports, football and boxing, that have spread the widest. There cannot be much doubt that the whole thing is bound up with the rise of nationalism – that is, with the lunatic modern habit of identifying oneself with large power units and seeing everything in terms of competitive prestige. Also, organised games are more likely to flourish in urban communities where the average human being lives a sedentary, or at least a confined, life, and does not get much opportunity for creative labour. Games are taken seriously in London and New York, and they were taken seriously in Rome and Byzantium: in the Middle Ages they were played, and probably played with much physical brutality, but they were not mixed up with politics, nor a cause of group hatreds.

EXERCISES

COMPREHENDING A

1. In your own words, explain the main argument that George Orwell makes in this article.
2. Do you agree or disagree with the view that *"serious sport has nothing to do with fair play"*? Give reasons for your answer.
3. Comment on the writer's success or otherwise in presenting a convincing case. You must refer to both style and content. Support with reference to the passage.

COMPREHENDING B

Write out the words of a team talk or speech that a captain or coach might give to his/her players before an important match or event.

TEXT 2

SPORTING IMAGES

EXERCISES

COMPREHENDING A

Take time to study these images and answer the following questions:

1. What overall image of sport is conveyed by these images? Support your answer with reference to the images.
2. Of the images, which one best illustrates the positive contribution made by sport? You must write a persuasive text for the reader about your choice.
3. What aspects of sport should have been included in this photographic display that have not been? Suggest two images you would have included and give reason for your choice.

COMPREHENDING B

Imagine you are a sports person competing in an international event. Write your blog or Internet diary for the days before and after your participation.

TEXT 3

Con Houlihan, a legendary sports writer, captures the famous victory of the Republic of Ireland over Italy during the 1994 World Cup. The match was played in New York.

THE 1994 WORLD CUP

On Saturday morning, I was reminded of a film which was a classic and is a classic and belongs to a generation ago. It was called *The Wages of Fear*. The principal characters were Yves Montand and Charles Vanel.

The story is set in a godforsaken town in Latin America where a small number of Europeans are desperate to get away to a better world. The chance comes when fire breaks out in an oilfield a few hundred miles away. Two truckloads of dynamite are needed to cut off the fire. The two drivers chosen are Montand and an actor whose name I have forgotten but whom I remember as being quintessentially Scandinavian.

They set off. Montand is a good distance in front. When the Scandinavian comes near journey's end, he shaves off his beard with enormous concentration as if he felt some momentous event was about to occur. A few miles down the road his lorry explodes and he dies clean.

On Saturday morning, another memory came back to me. It concerned the occasion of my First Holy Communion. I wasn't worried about the experience itself but about my clothes.

My mother had ordered a new suit; we had the jacket but the trousers weren't ready. And that morning as I went towards the town, I experienced for the first time in my life what I know as nervous tension.

I was terrified going up to the altar rails with my splendid new coat and pants that had known a long and hectic life worn by a small boy devoted to hunting hares and rabbits and winkling fish out of their watery homes. The pants were ready and all was well. That is all a very long time ago but on Saturday morning I felt a tension of a kind I hadn't known for years.

I was fearful that our football team would be devastated by Italy. And then all the great deeds of the past would be turned to dust and the great celebrations at Dublin Airport at the homecomings would look like fool's gold. Italy's team-sheet bristled with great names; at least six would be candidates for a world team and at least two, Paolo Maldini and Roberto Baggio, would be almost certainties. Some of our best team were perhaps a little beyond their best and others were very short of experience. I was thinking especially of Phil Babb; he had excelled in manoeuvres but I wondered how he would fare in war.

I was out at the stadium two hours before starting time. And the heat and humidity and the huge presence of Italians increased my fears. At last, the magnificent opening ceremony was over and the warfare began. After the first minute I knew that we wouldn't be devastated. Packie Bonner radiated confidence and Stephen Staunton fired in a shot that indicated that Republic weren't overawed.

Ten minutes later we saw Ray Houghton score a marvellous goal: from twenty-five yards he sent in a dipping shot that deceived Gianluca Pagliuca and went under his bar. The great keeper looked like a king who, though hedged by minders, found his pocket picked. This marvellous opening gave the Irish tremendous confidence and, backed by the great following, they took on the Italians in every department.

Our full-backs, Denis Irwin and Terry Phelan, were keeping house tidily and occasionally foraging into the big world outside. Phil Babb was playing with the coolness of a veteran and the zeal of a newcomer. And what can we say about Paul McGrath? In his long career he has never been more brilliant. He took the ball with every part of his foot: instep, side, heel and at times even sole. He looked as casual as if playing with his two small boys in his back garden. He was doing things that surely had Jack Charlton demented because our Jack likes things plain and simple.

Our Paul is a law unto himself. You cannot regulate genius. We were seeing

the gospel according to Paul. And in midfield we saw Andy Townsend and John Sheridan and Ray Houghton and Steve Staunton take on their illustrious counterparts and lose no caste. And while all this was going on, a young man from Cork called Roy Keane was hinting that soon he would be deemed a great master.

It was a marvellous game and we were thrilled to see our players hold their own in such illustrious company as Paolo Maldini and Franco Baresi and Roberto Baggio and Roberto Donadoni and Giuseppe Signori. The Republic dominated the first half. Then the Italians came out and put men forward and for about twenty minutes besieged Packie Bonner's goal. Our keeper excelled himself; he was in the heroic form which we saw in Stuttgart on that famous day when we beat England. And up in front Tommy Coyne was waging a great battle though outnumbered two to one. It all ended happily and for a long time I will remember my great friend Paul soaring to rule the sky and crouching to rule the earth.

By the way, the first truck of dynamite got to the oilfield and helped to quell the blaze – as Jack Charlton would say, they closed it down.

EXERCISES

COMPREHENDING A

1. What do you think is the purpose of the writer's reference to the film *Wages of Fear?* In your answer, comment on what it contributes to the passage.
2. *"It was a marvellous game."* Has the writer convinced you that it was a marvellous game? Support your answer with reference to the text.
3. Con Houlihan was a sportswriter who was read even by people who have little interest in sport. From the evidence of this extract, suggest reasons why this was so. You must refer to both the style and content of the extract.

COMPREHENDING B

Write an article for a popular magazine on the contribution that sport can make to society.

COMPOSING

1. *"Another memory came back to me."*
   Write a personal essay in which you explore your own sporting experiences.
2. Write out the text of a speech addressing the motion: "Sport has nothing to do with fair play." You can argue for or against the motion.
3. *"To play for fun."*
   Write an article persuading young people to participate in sport.
4. *"I was fearful."*
   Write a short story that is set five years after the main character won a major trophy.
5. *"You play to win."*
   Write a humorous article in which you chart your own sporting failures and successes.
6. *"I felt a tension I hadn't known for years."*
   Write a short story in which the main character is a sports writer.
7. *"It was marvellous and we were thrilled."*
   Write a descriptive essay outlining a scene of jubilation following an important sporting victory.

ENDINGS

TEXT 1

This passage is from the last page of James Joyce's short story 'The Dead'. The main character, Gabriel Conroy, and his wife Greta have just come back to their hotel having attended an annual Christmas party at his elderly aunt's house. Greta tells Gabriel that when she was a young girl in Galway she was in love with a boy, Michael Furey. She had decided to join the convent and become a nun. Young Michael was very sick. The night before she was due to leave, he left his sick bed, and sang a song to her from below her window. He died shortly later. In this passage, Greta has fallen asleep and Gabriel thinks about the story his wife has just told him. The story is set in Dublin.

THE DEAD

She was fast asleep.

Gabriel, leaning on his elbow, looked for a few moments unresentfully on her tangled hair and half-open mouth, listening to her deep-drawn breath. So she had had that romance in her life: a man had died for her sake. It hardly pained him now to think how poor a part he, her husband, had played in her life. He watched her while she slept, as though he and she had never lived together as man and wife. His curious eyes rested long upon her face and on her hair: and, as he thought of what she must have been then, in that time of her first girlish beauty, a strange, friendly pity for her entered his soul. He did not like

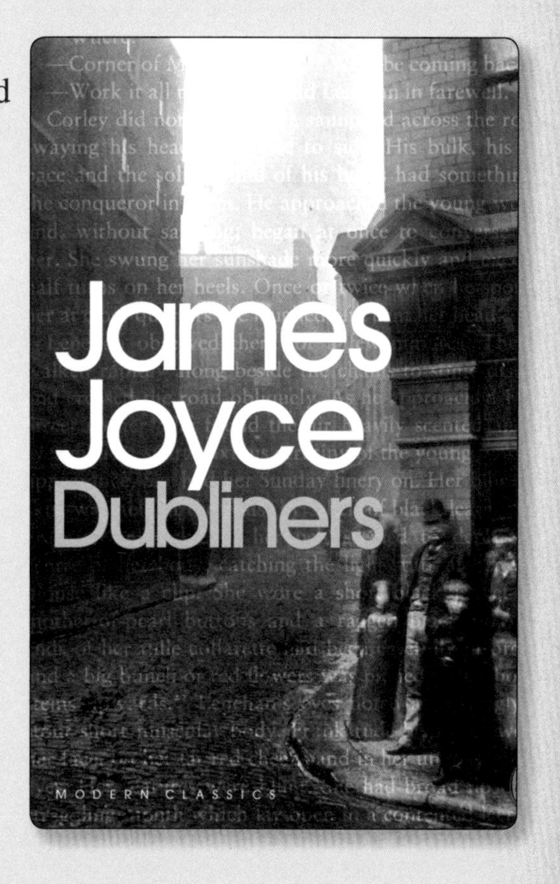

to say even to himself that her face was no longer beautiful, but he knew that it was no longer the face for which Michael Furey had braved death.

Perhaps she had not told him all the story. His eyes moved to the chair over which she had thrown some of her clothes. A petticoat string dangled to the floor. One boot stood upright, its limp upper fallen down: the fellow of it lay upon its side. He wondered at his riot of emotions of an hour before. From what had it proceeded? From his aunt's supper, from his own foolish speech, from the wine and dancing, the merrymaking when saying good night in the hall, the pleasure of the walk along the river in the snow. Poor Aunt Julia! She, too, would soon be a shade with the shade of Patrick Morkan and his horse. He had caught that haggard look upon her face for a moment when she was singing 'Arrayed for the Bridal'. Soon, perhaps, he would be sitting in that same drawing-room, dressed in black, his silk hat on his knees. The blinds would be drawn down and Aunt Kate would be sitting beside him, crying and blowing her nose and telling him how Julia had died. He would cast about in his mind for some words that might console her, and would find only lame and useless ones. Yes, yes: that would happen very soon.

The air of the room chilled his shoulders. He stretched himself cautiously along under the sheets and lay down beside his wife. One by one, they were all becoming shades. Better pass boldly into that other world, in the full glory of some passion, than fade and wither dismally with age. He thought of how she who lay beside him had locked in her heart for so many years that image of her lover's eyes when he had told her that he did not wish to live.

Generous tears filled Gabriel's eyes. He had never felt like that himself towards any woman, but he knew that such feeling must be love. The tears gathered more thickly in his eyes and in the partial darkness he imagined he saw the form of a young man standing under a dripping tree. Other forms were near. His soul had approached that region where dwell the vast hosts of the dead. He was conscious of, but could not apprehend, their wayward and flickering existence. His own identity was fading out into a grey impalpable world: the solid world itself, which these dead had one time reared and lived in, was dissolving and dwindling.

A few light taps upon the pane made him turn to the window. It had begun to snow again. He watched sleepily the flakes, silver and dark, falling obliquely against the lamp-light. The time had come for him to set out on his journey westward. Yes, the newspapers were right: snow was general all over Ireland. It was falling on every part of the dark central plain, on the treeless hills, falling softly upon the Bog of Allen and, farther westward, softly falling into the dark mutinous Shannon waves. It was falling, too, upon every part of the lonely churchyard on the hill where Michael Furey lay buried. It lay thickly drifted on the crooked crosses and headstones, on the spears of the little gate, on the barren thorns. His soul swooned slowly as he heard the snow falling faintly through the universe and faintly falling, like the descent of their last end, upon all the living and the dead.

EXERCISES

COMPREHENDING A

1. What impression do you have of the character of Gabriel Conroy? You must support your answer with reference to the text.
2. Identify and comment on **four** features of descriptive writing evident in this passage. Support your answer by illustration from the text.
3. Is this a story you would normally like to read? You must support your answer with reference to the text.

COMPREHENDING B

You have been asked to write a speech for a New Year's radio broadcast. Write out the text of the speech you would deliver.

TEXT 2

Martin Luther King was shot dead on the 4 April 1968. He spent his life campaigning for civil rights. This speech was delivered the night before he was killed.

THE LAST NIGHT

You know, several years ago, I was in New York City autographing the first book that I had written. And while sitting there autographing books, a demented black woman came up. The only question I heard from her was, "Are you Martin Luther King?"

And I was looking down writing, and I said yes. And the next minute I felt something beating on my chest. Before I knew it I had been stabbed by this demented woman. I was rushed to Harlem Hospital. It was a dark Saturday afternoon. And that blade had gone through, and the X-rays revealed that the tip of the blade was on the edge of my aorta, the main artery. And once that's punctured, you drown in your own blood – that's the end of you.

It came out in the *New York Times* the next morning, that if I had sneezed, I would have died. Well, about four days later, they allowed me, after the operation, after my chest had been opened, and the blade had been taken out, to move around in the wheel chair in the hospital. They allowed me to read some of the mail that came in, and from all over the states, and the world, kind letters came in. I read a few, but one of them I will never forget. I had received one from the President and the Vice President. I've forgotten what those telegrams said. I'd received a visit and a letter from the Governor of New York, but I've forgotten what the letter said. But there was another letter that came from a little girl, a young girl who

was a student at the White Plains High School. And I looked at that letter, and I'll never forget it. It said simply, "Dear Dr King: I am a ninth-grade student at the White Plains High School." She said, "While it should not matter, I would like to mention that I am a white girl. I read in the paper of your misfortune, and of your suffering. And I read that if you had sneezed, you would have died. And I'm simply writing to you that I'm so happy that you didn't sneeze."

And I want to say tonight, I want to say that I am happy that I didn't sneeze. Because if I had sneezed, I wouldn't have been around here in 1960, when students all over the South started sitting-in at lunch counters. And I knew that as they were sitting in, they were really standing up for the best in the American dream. And taking the whole nation back to those great wells of democracy which were dug deep by the Founding Fathers in the Declaration of Independence and the Constitution. If I had sneezed, I wouldn't have been around in 1962, when Negroes in Albany, Georgia, decided to straighten their backs up. And whenever men and women straighten their backs up, they are going somewhere, because a man can't ride your back unless it is bent. If I had sneezed, I wouldn't have been here in 1963, when the black people of Birmingham, Alabama, aroused the conscience of this nation, and brought into being the Civil Rights Bill. If I had sneezed, I wouldn't have had a chance later that year, in August, to try to tell America about a dream that I had had. If I had sneezed, I wouldn't have been down in Selma, Alabama, to see the great movement there. If I had sneezed, I wouldn't have been in Memphis to see a community rally around those brothers and sisters who are suffering. I'm so happy I didn't sneeze.

And they were telling me, now it doesn't matter now. It really doesn't matter what happens now. I left Atlanta this morning, and as we got started on the plane, there were six of us, the pilot said over the public address system, "We are sorry for the delay, but we have Dr Martin Luther King on the plane. And to be sure that all of the bags were checked, and to be sure that nothing would be wrong with the plane, we had to check out everything carefully. And we've had the plane protected and guarded all night."

And then I got into Memphis. And some began to say that threats, or talk about the threats that were out. What would happen to me from some of our sick white brothers?

Well, I don't know what will happen now. We've got some difficult days ahead. But it doesn't matter with me now. Because I've been to the mountaintop. And I don't mind. Like anybody, I would like to have a long life. Longevity has its place. But I'm not concerned about that now. I just want to do God's will. And He's allowed me to go up to the mountain. And I've looked over. And I've seen the promised land. I may not get there with you. But I want you to know tonight, that we, as a people will get to the promised land. And I'm happy, tonight. I'm not worried about anything. I'm not fearing any man. Mine eyes have seen the glory of the coming of the Lord.

EXERCISES

COMPREHENDING A

1. Read the first three paragraphs. How effective are they as an opening for a speech? You must give reasons for your answer.
2. What is your reaction to this speech in the light of the fact that this was the last speech given by Martin Luther King? Support your answer with reference to the text.
3. Identify and comment on the main features of style that make this a powerful speech. Support with references to the text.

COMPREHENDING B

Write a letter to a national newspaper on a human rights' issue that you think needs to be addressed.

TEXT 3

HERE LIES

These poems are taken from a book called The Spoon River Anthology *written by Edgar Lee Masters. The entire work is set in a cemetery. Each poem is in the voice of a character speaking to us from his/her grave. The poems reveal secrets about the characters and the town.*

JUDGE SELAH LIVELY

Suppose you stood just five feet two,
And had worked your way as a grocery clerk,
Studying law by the candle light
Until you became an attorney at law?
And then suppose through your diligence,
And regular church attendance,
You became attorney for Thomas Rhodes,
Collecting notes and mortgages,
And representing all the widows
In the Probate Court? And through it all
They jeered at your size, and laughed at your clothes
And your polished boots? And then suppose
You became the County Judge?
And Jefferson Howard and Kinsey Keene,
And Harmon Whitney, and all the giants
Who had sneered at you, were forced to stand
Before the bar and say "Your Honor" –
Well, don't you think it was natural
That I made it hard for them?

WALTER SIMMONS

My parents thought that I would be
As great as Edison or greater:
For as a boy I made balloons
And wondrous kites and toys with clocks
And little engines with tracks to run on
And telephones of cans and thread.

I played the cornet and painted pictures,
Modeled in clay and took the part
Of the villain in the Octoroon
But then at twenty-one I married
And had to live, and so, to live
I learned the trade of making watches
And kept the jewelry store on the square,
Thinking, thinking, thinking, –
Not of business, but of the engine
I studied the calculus to build.
And all Spoon River watched and waited
To see it work, but it never worked.
And a few kind souls believed my genius
Was somehow hampered by the store.
It wasn't true. The truth was this:
I didn't have the brains.

ELSA WERTMAN

I was a peasant girl from Germany,
Blue-eyed, rosy, happy and strong.
And the first place I worked was at Thomas Greene's.
On a summer's day when she was away
He stole into the kitchen and took me
Right in his arms and kissed me on my throat,
I turning my head. Then neither of us
Seemed to know what happened.
And I cried for what would become of me.
And cried and cried as my secret began to show.
One day Mrs Greene said she understood,
And would make no trouble for me,
And, being childless, would adopt it.
(He had given her a farm to be still).
So she hid in the house and sent out rumors,
As if it were going to happen to her.
And all went well and the child was born – They were so kind to me,
Later I married Gus Wertman, and years passed.
But – at political rallies when sitters-by thought I was crying
At the eloquence of Hamilton Greene –
That was not it.
No! I wanted to say:
That's my son! That's my son!

VISUALS

DIANA SPENCER

SYLVIA PLATH

WAR CEMETERY

W.B. YEATS

EXERCISES

COMPREHENDING A

1. Read the three poems taken from *The Spoon River Anthology.* Write your personal reaction to the one that you find the most moving. You must explain your choice.
2. Having read the three poems, would you agree that they give us a special insight into the secret world of life in a small town? In your answer, refer to what you learnt about life in the town.
3. Study the visuals. Choose one that has affected you most. Give reasons for your choice.

COMPREHENDING B

A teacher or pupil is leaving the school due to unforeseen circumstances. Write a farewell speech to be delivered to your school assembly.

COMPOSING

1. *"Tears filled Gabriel's eyes."*
   Write a personal essay in which you explore your reflections upon your grandparents and relatives that have been important to you growing up.
2. Write a short story that begins with the words: *"The light in the graveyard was growing dim..."*
3. *"It had begun to snow again..."*
   Write an essay describing the last day of the year.
4. You have been asked to write a speech on the motion: *"The world today lacks role models that inspire young people"*. You may argue for or against the motion.
5. *"I just want to do God's will."*
   Write a personal reflection on how you would like to be remembered.
6. Write a short story which is inspired by the title *'Endings'*.
7. *"The truth was this: I didn't have the brains."*
   Write a story in which the main character narrates events from beyond the grave. There should be an element of surprise in the story.

Notes

Notes